Mutual Funds

D0830293

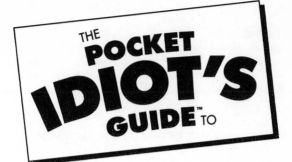

Mutual Funds

by Lita Epstein, MBA

ALPHA

A member of Penguin Group (USA) Inc.

ALPHA BOOKS

Published by the Penguin Group

Penguin Group (USA) Inc., 375 Hudson Street, New York, New York 10014, USA

Penguin Group (Canada), 90 Eglinton Avenue East, Suite 700, Toronto, Ontario M4P 2Y3, Canada (a division of Pearson Penguin Canada Inc.)

Penguin Books Ltd., 80 Strand, London WC2R 0RL, England

Penguin Ireland, 25 St. Stephen's Green, Dublin 2, Ireland (a division of Penguin Books Ltd.)

Penguin Group (Australia), 250 Camberwell Road, Camberwell, Victoria 3124, Australia (a division of Pearson Australia Group Pty. Ltd.)

Penguin Books India Pvt. Ltd., 11 Community Centre, Panchsheel Park, New Delhi—110 017, India

Penguin Group (NZ), 67 Apollo Drive, Rosedale, North Shore, Auckland 1311, New Zealand (a division of Pearson New Zealand Ltd.)

Penguin Books (South Africa) (Pty.) Ltd., 24 Sturdee Avenue, Rosebank, Johannesburg 2196, South Africa

Penguin Books Ltd., Registered Offices: 80 Strand, London WC2R 0RL, England

International Standard Book Number: 978-1-59257-630-2
Library of Congress Catalog Card Number: 2006940220

09 08 07   8 7 6 5 4 3 2 1

Interpretation of the printing code: The rightmost number of the first series of numbers is the year of the book's printing; the rightmost number of the second series of numbers is the number of the book's printing. For example, a printing code of 07-1 shows that the first printing occurred in 2007.

Printed in the United States of America

Note: This publication contains the opinions and ideas of its author. It is intended to provide helpful and informative material on the subject matter covered. It is sold with the understanding that the author and publisher are not engaged in rendering professional services in the book. If the reader requires personal assistance or advice, a competent professional should be consulted.

The author and publisher specifically disclaim any responsibility for any liability, loss, or risk, personal or otherwise, which is incurred as a consequence, directly or indirectly, of the use and application of any of the contents of this book.

Most Alpha books are available at special quantity discounts for bulk purchases for sales promotions, premiums, fund-raising, or educational use. Special books, or book excerpts, can also be created to fit specific needs.

For details, write: Special Markets, Alpha Books, 375 Hudson Street, New York, NY 10014.

Contents

Introduction

Mutual funds can be an ideal investment vehicle for all types of investors, from beginners to experienced.

If you're a beginner, it gives you a way to get started in investing and to build a diversified portfolio with the help of a professional manager. Even if you only have a few hundred dollars to begin building that stock portfolio, you don't have to wait. You don't have to risk all your money by buying just one stock, either. Instead, you can own a part of hundreds of stocks by choosing a mutual fund.

If you're an experienced investor, it gives you a way to build and manage a diversified portfolio without worrying every day about the ups and downs of a large group of stocks and bonds you hold individually. Your time is freed up for doing other things that you enjoy doing.

While some experienced investors do enjoy all the time it takes to research and pick their own stocks and bonds and then monitor each stock or bond's performance, for many people this can be more of a burden than a joy. Mutual funds take this responsibility away from the investor who doesn't really enjoy spending his time reading all the news, digesting all the analysis, and worrying about when to buy and sell his individual stocks and bonds.

Instead of spending hours or days managing a portfolio of individual stocks and bonds, you can spend a few hours two or three times a year reviewing the performance of the 5 to 10 mutual funds you hold. Mutual funds are the closest you can get to putting your portfolio on autopilot and letting it build.

In this book, we start by introducing you to the world of mutual funds and explaining why they make a great investment vehicle. Then we explore the various types of mutual funds from which you can choose.

After that we review the mechanics of how to invest in mutual funds and discuss the fees you must pay and how to minimize them. We explore the strategies you can employ to build and manage a mutual fund portfolio that best matches your investment goals. Then we discuss the unique tax rules that mutual fund owners face. And finally we talk about how to fix any administrative problems you might have with your mutual fund portfolio.

Enjoy your journey learning about the world of mutual funds. Then start building your own dreams by investing through just the right mutual funds for you and your family.

Extras

We've developed a few helpers you'll find in little boxes throughout the book:

def•i•ni•tion

These help you learn the language of mutual funds.

Fund Fears

These give you warnings about things you need to avoid.

Fund Facts

These help you explore additional information about key mutual fund topics.

Mutual Aids

These give you ideas for setting up your mutual fund portfolio and finding the resources you need.

Acknowledgments

I want to thank Paul Dinas, my acquisitions editor, for his constant support and help. I also want to thank Julie Bess for her efforts as development editor in getting this completed, as well as Megan Douglass, production editor, for all her help in getting things done.

Trademarks

All terms mentioned in this book that are known to be or are suspected of being trademarks or service marks have been appropriately capitalized. Alpha Books and Penguin Group (USA) Inc. cannot attest to the accuracy of this information. Use of a term in this book should not be regarded as affecting the validity of any trademark or service mark.

Why Invest in Mutual Funds?

In This Chapter

- Defining funds
- A look at the advantages
- Depend on the pros
- A review of the risks
- Recognizing the disadvantages

More than 90 million people in the United States choose mutual funds as their way to invest in stocks, bonds, and money market instruments. By the end of 2005, more than $8.9 trillion had been invested through mutual funds. The largest chunk of these investments, $3.4 trillion, have been purchased as part of employer-sponsored retirement savings plans or for individual retirement accounts (IRA).

As a small investor, when you use mutual funds, you get an excellent diversified vehicle through which you can participate in the financial markets with very little cash up front. For example, you can start a mutual fund account with as little as $250 or $500 with some mutual fund companies. You also get affordable access to a diversified portfolio managed by a professional financial portfolio manager.

In this chapter, we explain what a mutual fund is and explore the advantages of investing this way. In addition, we discuss the risks you'll face and alert you to the disadvantages of investing through mutual funds.

What Is a Mutual Fund?

Mutual funds pool the money of many individual investors and then invest those funds in a variety of ways. A mutual fund manager combines the funds from all these individual investors into a portfolio, which can be made up of stocks, bonds, and/or money market instruments (which can include savings accounts, certificate of deposits, and money market funds).

How that portfolio is actually constructed depends upon a set of stated objectives. These objectives include the goal of the fund, the types of investments that can be included in the portfolio, and the country or countries in which the mutual fund can invest.

In Chapter 5, we explain about researching funds and writing the objectives of a fund. In Chapters 6 and 7, we talk about mutual fund investment strategies and the constructing of your own fund portfolio.

But before we can talk about strategy, you first need to understand the types of mutual funds (Chapter 2) and the mechanics of investing in those funds.

Chapter 3 reviews the logistics of how to invest in funds. And Chapter 4 digs into the commissions and fees you must pay and explains ways to minimize those fees.

Exploring the Advantages of Investing Through Mutual Funds

Mutual funds offer many advantages, including instant diversification of your investments, marketability, convenience, flexibility, and variety. So let's consider these key advantages of mutual fund investing.

Mixing It Up—Diversification

How well you diversify and balance your portfolio by owning a good mix of stocks and bonds is the most important decision any investor can make. You can reduce your risks, as well as the volatility of your portfolio, by properly diversifying it.

Because many small investors just don't have enough money to properly diversify their portfolios, mutual funds offer the small investor instant *diversification* because they can pool their assets with other investors.

This diversification reduces the risks and volatility of investing directly in stocks or bonds of individual companies. The stocks or bonds chosen for a mutual fund's portfolio are made either by a professional manager or by using a mathematical model called *indexing*.

def•i•ni•tion

Diversification is a strategy used to reduce your exposure to risk by holding a variety of investments, such as stocks, bonds, and real estate, which don't usually move up or down in value in the same direction at the same time. By diversifying your portfolio, if one type of investment is going up and another type is going down, your total portfolio value will be less volatile.

Indexing is a portfolio management tool in which a computerized program is used to match the performance of a particular stock or bond index. For example, the Dow Jones Industrial Average is an index of 30 key stocks and the Standard & Poor's 500 is an index of 500 key stocks.

As a mutual fund shareholder, you will own a portion of the portfolio and get distributions in the form of dividends, interest, and/or capital gains (profits made on the sale of an asset) based on this share. You can build your portfolio even more quickly by automatically reinvesting these distributions.

Mutual Aids

Mutual funds offer you instant diversification. Even if you have only $500
to invest, you can own a piece of 100
different shares of stocks when you buy a
mutual fund.

Marketability

If you invest directly by buying stocks, bonds, or
even real estate, you always run the risk of not
being able to sell the asset when you need the
funds. When you invest using mutual funds, you
don't have to worry about that.

By law, a mutual fund company must be able to buy
back your assets by the end of the day you want to
sell. If you need the money quickly, you can even
make arrangements to have the money wired to
your checking account the next day, or you can have
the funds transferred to a money market fund in the
same fund family and write a check based on the
funds deposited.

Convenience

You can use many different means to buy and sell
mutual funds. Funds can be bought and sold by
mail, phone, or electronic transfer. You can buy
them through a broker, your bank, an insurance
agent, or directly from the mutual fund company
that is selling the funds.

To make investing even easier, you can arrange for automatic monthly deposits from your paycheck or bank account. You can let your money grow more rapidly by automatically reinvesting your dividends and capital gains. We talk more about the mechanics of buying and selling funds in Chapter 3.

Flexibility

You don't have to worry about picking the wrong fund. If you're not happy with the performance of a fund, you can easily move funds from one mutual fund to another.

Sometimes you may want to switch to another fund in the same fund family. Often you can do this by telephone or online because many mutual fund companies allow you to transfer funds using their website. If you've done online banking, you'll find that working with mutual fund company websites is very similar.

If you buy funds through a broker, he or she will gladly handle any transfer of funds for you. Many discount brokers also provide online access so you can easily switch your holdings from one mutual fund to another. You'll learn more about brokers in Chapter 3.

Variety

Variety is the spice of life, and there is no shortage of it when investing using mutual funds. With over 8,000 mutual funds offered by approximately 700 mutual fund families, you can find a mutual fund that matches just about any investing strategy you select.

You'll find funds that focus on blue-chip stocks, technology stocks, bonds, socially responsible companies, or the country of your choosing. The greatest challenge can be sorting through the variety and picking the best mutual funds for you. As you read through these chapters, you'll learn how to begin the daunting task of selecting the right funds for you.

Getting Help from Professionals

If you're a beginning investor, mutual funds give you the best of both worlds—a way to diversify your portfolio plus professional advice for managing that portfolio. While some analysts may tell you that professional management is not necessarily an advantage, a good money manager is certainly worth the fees you will pay.

 Mutual Aids

> Even if you have enough money to properly diversify your portfolio, you would need extensive knowledge as well as be able to spend full time researching the companies you select to manage your own portfolio as effectively as a professional manager.

You do need to take the time to research the managers, though, to be sure you are finding the best ones. Good mutual fund managers with an excellent research team can do a better job of monitoring the companies they have chosen to invest in than you can.

When you buy a mutual fund, the primary asset you are buying is the manager who will be controlling which assets are chosen to meet the fund's stated investment objectives. So, in addition to looking at a fund manager's credentials, look at the fund manager's tenure as well. Sometimes a manager who has left the fund built the excellent performance track record you see for a mutual fund. We'll talk more about researching funds and their fund managers in Chapter 5.

You will find two types of mutual fund managers, passive and active. Here are the differences:

Passive Mutual Fund Management

Passively managed funds are index funds. Mutual fund indexing attempts to match the returns of a particular stock or bond index, such as the Dow Industrial Index.

The investment advisor managing the fund seeks to replicate the target index by holding all or a representative sample of the stocks or bonds that make up the target index. There is no attempt to actively manage the funds or buy a large number of shares in any individual company to outperform the market.

Many times investment choices are done using a software program developed specifically to match the index. Assets for the fund are bought and sold based on this computer software.

Fund Facts

John C. Bogle created the first index mutual fund in 1976 when he introduced the First Index Investment Trust. Today that fund is the largest and most successful index fund—Vanguard 500 Index.

John Bogle has since retired from Vanguard, but his fund and the company he started are still one of the top mutual funds and mutual fund companies in the United States. Today Vanguard offers the largest selection of low-cost index funds on the market.

The indexing theory of investments is based on three key aspects:

- Investing is a zero-sum game. If one investor does better than the market, another must underperform.
- Costs of mutual fund investing lowers investors' returns because the benchmark index has no costs. By minimizing mutual fund costs, more money remains in investors' accounts.
- Financial markets are efficient, with information flowing freely. This makes it more difficult for a fund manager to consistently outperform over the long term.

Active Mutual Fund Management

A mutual fund manager who actively manages his fund attempts to do better than the market. He works to outperform the market by selecting stock in the companies he believes will do better than the rest of the market.

Investing using actively managed mutual funds can be very rewarding but requires a great deal of research. Even after you select your fund, you must spend time monitoring your funds for changes in mutual fund manager, management structure, and investment strategies.

Remember this key point whenever you are investing in mutual funds: when you buy a mutual fund, the primary asset you are buying is the manager who will be controlling assets in the fund.

While index funds are managed using a computer program that alerts the management team when to buy and sell funds to match the index, decision making for actively managed mutual funds is more subjective. There is more dependence on the knowledge and skills of the manager and his research team, so careful selection of a manager is important.

Knowing Your Risks

When thinking about investments, many people make the mistake of only considering market risk—the ups and downs of the market. While this definitely is a factor you'll need to consider, many more risks are involved in any type of investing. These risks impact your portfolio in various ways, but mutual fund investing helps minimize them.

Inflation Risk

If you are someone who is afraid to take risks, you'll most likely feel the impact of inflation risk. The risk here is that your money will not be worth as much in the future because its value will be eaten up by inflation.

As you are well aware, the costs of the basics of life increase every year—housing, clothing, medical care, gas, and food. By investing solely through guaranteed fixed-rate investment alternatives (such as certificates of deposits or savings accounts), you won't be able to keep up with inflation.

These fixed-income investments often offer interest rates that are below the annual inflation rate. For example, if your savings account is paying just 2 percent interest and the inflation rate is 4 percent, you will actually lose 2 percent in the value of your portfolio to inflation.

Opportunity Risk

Opportunity risk is the risk of trade-offs. When you choose to buy one type of investment, you are making the choice not to buy another. Or while your money is tied up in one investment, you may not have the cash to invest in something else. Missing an investment because your cash is tied up somewhere else is a type of opportunity risk.

For example, if you invest in long-term bonds and certificates of deposit, you are most likely to face this situation at some point. Suppose you tie up your funds in a 10-year certificate of deposit (CD) at 4 percent and interest rates rise to 7 percent. You are stuck for 10 years, or you must pay a penalty to get out of the CD early.

A bond's opportunity risk can be even greater than a CD's. For example, if you buy a 10-year bond and you later want to get out early to take advantage of an increase in interest rates, you likely will have to sell the bond below its face value and take a loss.

A mutual fund that invests primarily in bonds helps you minimize this risk because the fund holds many different types of bonds with each paying different interest rates. So even if some of the bonds in the fund lose value as interest rates rise, others that have higher interest rates won't lose value. The diversity of bond holdings helps you minimize opportunity risk.

Reinvestment Risk

Whenever you buy a fixed-rate investment, such as a bond or CD, you run the risk of not being able to reinvest your funds at the same earnings rate when the investment matures.

For example, suppose you invested in a bond paying 7 percent that matures in 10 years. When the 10 years are up, you find interest rates have dropped to 5 percent. What will you then do with your principal?

Mutual funds minimize this reinvestment risk because your mutual fund portfolio holds many different bonds or other fixed investments that mature (come due) at various times. Portfolio managers can more easily diversify their holdings because they have a much larger pool of funds to work with than you would have as an individual investor buying an individual bond.

Concentration Risk

You can probably recognize concentration risk from a phrase that's frequently used to describe it—"don't put all your eggs in one basket." Diversifying your investments is the best way to avoid this risk.

Mutual funds are an excellent way of diversifying your portfolio and taking advantage of professional management, even if you are starting with a very small nest egg.

Interest Rate Risk

If you watch the Fed's proclamations of interest rate changes and the impact they have on the market, this risk becomes very visible. Bonds feel the bite immediately. As interest rates rise, bond prices fall.

The reaction in the stock market will vary depending upon how interest rates affect the particular industry or company involved. Companies that carry a lot of debt are greatly impacted by this risk.

Again, since your mutual fund holds many different stocks and bonds, you won't be impacted as severely with interest rate changes. The diversity of the portfolio will mean that some of your holdings will go up and some will go down, but the total portfolio value will not be as volatile as it would have been if you were holding only an individual stock or bond that went down dramatically in value.

Credit or Default Risk

Every day of the week some borrowers don't have the money to repay a loan or bond obligation. This is known as credit or default risk.

Banks face this risk every day, but you won't have to worry about it unless you invest in a mutual fund that holds junk bonds. A bond fund with a high yield may look very attractive to you, but the reason for that higher yield is the risk of the low-quality assets it holds.

Marketability Risk

Sometimes you may not be able to sell your investment when you want to, which is called marketability risk. Luckily, by using mutual funds, this is one risk you will not have to face because, as we mentioned earlier, mutual funds, by law, must have the ability to buy back your shares at the end of any business day.

You are more likely to face this risk in trying to sell real estate or the stock of a small company that is not heavily traded.

Currency Translation Risk

If you decide to buy international mutual funds, you may be exposed to currency translation risk.

Essentially, the value of your investment changes as the dollar rises and falls relative to the country or countries in which your mutual fund invests.

This is a major risk when investing in international mutual funds. In these funds, you face both market risk and the risk that the value of the dollar will fall against the currency of the countries where the fund holds assets.

Understanding the Cons

Nothing is perfect, and because there are some disadvantages to investing through mutual funds, we need to explore these negative aspects.

Funds Are Not Guaranteed

Remember mutual funds are not insured. The risk you take when investing through mutual funds tends to mirror the type of assets held in the mutual fund portfolio. While a mutual fund's diversity can minimize some of these risks, it can't eliminate them.

For example, aggressive stock funds will most likely experience losses similar to those experienced by aggressive stocks. The losses likely won't be as great as if you have invested in one or two aggressive stocks that both lost most of their value. Hopefully the aggressive growth stock fund you chose diversified its holdings well, and you won't lose a large chunk of your portfolio if one or two stocks drop in value.

But we don't recommend putting all your holdings in one mutual fund. You should diversify your
fund choices better than that. We'll talk more about
developing your investment strategy and picking
funds that match that strategy in Chapters 6 and 7.

Fund Fears

The U.S. Securities and Exchange
commission extensively regulates the
mutual fund industry, which is required to
disclose information about their fees, past
performance, and portfolio investments.
But no mutual fund company can guarantee that you won't lose your money when
you invest through that mutual fund.

Minimum Investment

All mutual funds require you to put in a minimum
amount to get started. This can be a big stumbling
block for many small investors. The most common
minimum initial investment is $2,500, but it can be
as high as $100,000 or more.

But don't despair. You can get started with as little
as $500, or $250, or as little as $100, if you agree to
make regular deposits of at least $50 a month. We
explain how to start small in Chapter 3.

Sales Charges and Ongoing Fees

If you choose to buy a fund through a broker, you
will need to pay a load, which is essentially a sales

commission that goes to the broker. This fee is taken right up front before your money is even deposited in the fund.

Mutual fund loads typically range from 3 percent to 8.5 percent. Some companies hide this load by putting it on the back end when you sell. Other fees you need to carefully research are management and operating fees, 12b-1 (or marketing) costs, transaction fees, and redemption fees. We talk more about commissions and fees in Chapter 4.

No Local Branch Offices

You can't easily walk into a mutual fund office and ask to talk with someone, unless you just happen to live where the mutual fund is headquartered. Mutual funds work with their customers by phone, by mail, online, or at regional service centers.

Keeping Records and Tracking Performance

Keeping meticulous records of fund transactions is critical. You must carefully track your mutual fund purchases, as well as any reinvestments. That way you will know what your cost basis is when you decide to sell the fund.

You need this cost basis in order to report any sales of your funds. You must pay capital gains tax on any mutual fund profits, so you want to be able to show what your initial buying costs were. That way you can subtract all your purchase costs to reduce your profit and the capital gains tax you'll need to pay.

Tracking performance requires more time than just watching the fund price in the newspapers. You must carefully monitor manager and management changes to be certain the fund still meets your objectives and is still being managed the way you want.

Now that you have an idea about how the world of mutual funds works, let's continue into the next chapter and take a look at the different types of mutual funds available on the market today.

The Least You Need to Know

- Mutual fund investing is the perfect choice for the small investor because he can pool funds with other small investors and have enough money to be part of a well-diversified investment portfolio.

- In addition to diversification, the advantages of investing in mutual funds include market-ability, convenience, flexibility, and variety.

- You do take risks when you invest through mutual funds, but those risks are minimized with a well-diversified, professionally man-aged portfolio.

- Mutual funds are not insured, as your funds would be with a bank that offers insurance, so you could lose your money.

Chapter

Discovering Mutual Fund Types

In This Chapter

- Consider the stock
- Building bonds
- Making money
- Balanced funds
- Cycling through life

As you begin to explore the world of mutual funds, you'll find more than 8,000 mutual funds on the market. How can you possibly choose among that many?

Luckily, mutual funds are grouped by the type of investment vehicles you might want to use—stocks, bonds, or cash—as well as by their investment goals. These groupings help you pick the type of funds you want based on the fund's investing style.

In this chapter, we review the various types of mutual funds you can choose from and what types of investment vehicles you will find in each.

Stock

Stock funds invest primarily in common stocks that are found on the New York Stock Exchange, NASDAQ, American Stock Exchange, or other exchanges around the globe. A number of different categories of stock funds will help you quickly determine the investing style of a mutual fund's *portfolio manager*. The four key categories are:

- Growth
- Value
- Sector (funds focused on one industry)
- International

So let's talk about the types of stocks you would likely find in each type of portfolio.

def•i•ni•tion

The **portfolio manager** is the person in charge of picking the investments for the fund and managing those investments. When you buy a mutual fund, what you are really buying are the professional management skills of the portfolio manager. The portfolio manager is the one that buys the fund's assets.

Growth

Growth funds concentrate on the increase in value of the money you've invested or your *capital appreciation.* This can happen in two ways: the price of the stock held in the mutual fund portfolio goes up, which makes the portfolio more valuable, or profits are earned when selling a stock that goes up in value. Profits made when a stock is sold are called *capital gains.*

def•i•ni•tion

Capital appreciation is the increase in the current market value of your holdings. The market value is the price you can get for your asset if you want to sell it today.

Capital gains are the amount of profit you make when you sell an asset. For example, if you buy a share of stock for $10 and sell it for $15, your capital gain is $5 minus any fees or commissions you paid to buy and sell that stock.

Growth managers don't look for stocks that pay hefty dividends. Instead they want companies that have strong earnings potential that will drive the stock price up quickly.

In the growth fund category you will find two types of investing strategy—aggressive growth funds and growth funds. The most volatile type of mutual fund that comes with the greatest risk is the aggressive growth fund.

You'll usually find aggressive growth funds in the top 10 performers for the year, as well as in the list of the 10 worst performers for the year. You will often find that the top 10 performers in any one year will be near the bottom 10 the next year, so don't pick your funds solely by choosing those in the top 10.

 Fund Fears

Aggressive mutual funds are the most volatile. You often will find an aggressive mutual fund at the top of the list for any one year and then near the bottom of the list the next year. For example, ProFunds Ultra Japan Investors was the top performer in 2005 with a gain of 90.6%, then gained only 0.4 percent in 2006, putting it near the bottom of what was otherwise a very good year. If you held the fund before 2005, you'd be very happy, but if you bought the fund after you saw it at the top near the end of 2005, you'd see a return of just 0.4 percent in 2006—worse than most savings accounts in a bank.

When you pick an aggressive stock fund, expect a wild ride. One year you'll be at the top of the ladder with huge gains and the next year you could be near the bottom with a large loss. You must have a lot of patience for this type of fund and have the risk tolerance to ride out the lows in order to take advantage of the highs. If you don't, you'll probably end up selling the fund at one of its lows and lose a lot of money because you're too nervous to wait for a rebound.

The types of investments you'll find in aggressive growth stock funds include companies in developing industries and small but potentially fast-moving companies. These funds also tend to use speculative strategies, such as *options*, *futures*, and considerable *leverage*, to give fund owners a chance for significant and rapid gains, but you also risk significant and rapid losses as well.

def•i•ni•tion

Options and futures are speculative contracts that stock traders use to make money by betting on where the market may be headed. Leverage is borrowing money in order to buy an asset.

Growth fund managers also seek capital appreciation, but use much less aggressive tactics. These funds are not as volatile as aggressive growth funds. Growth fund portfolio managers will build their portfolios with well-established companies from industries with long-term growth potential rather than small emerging companies or developing industries.

Your potential for gains is not as high when you buy growth stock mutual funds as it would be with aggressive growth stocks, but your risk for loss also is much lower. You could lose some principal value in a bad year, but as long as you can hold the fund for the long term, you do have a good possibility of seeing sizeable gains.

Fund Fears

Don't expect much in the way of income from aggressive growth or growth stocks. Growth companies don't usually pay dividends; instead they reinvest their money in growing the company.

Value

Value funds, also known as growth and income funds, seek both long-term growth and current income. Current income is earned from *dividends* or interest, which are used to offset the volatility that you'll find in growth funds as the price of the stocks in the fund's portfolio goes up and down. Dividends and interest can stabilize the returns for these funds, even though capital gains will be more volatile.

def•i•ni•tion

Dividends are paid by a corporation to their stockholders based on the profits earned in a given year. This is the way corporations share their profits with the people who hold their stock.

Not all value funds are managed in the same way. Some managers concentrate on building their portfolios by picking stocks of well-established companies that pay significant dividends. Other managers put together a combination of growth stocks, stocks paying high dividends, *preferred stocks*, *convertible securities*, or fixed-income securities, such as corporate bonds and money market instruments.

def•i•ni•tion

Preferred stocks have a specified dividend that must be paid before common stock holders get their dividends. **Convertible securities** are bonds, preferred stock, or some other type of debt that can be converted to common stock.

Another common investing strategy for value managers is to look for beaten-down companies that have a good chance for recovery. Others might use a more aggressive tactic by using hedging strategies, such as investing in growth stocks and then buying and selling options to generate the income side of the portfolio rather than depending on dividends.

You will find that value funds are the least volatile of the stock fund group, as long as you find a good manager. I talk more about how to research funds in Chapter 5.

Sector

Sector fund managers concentrate their holdings in one specific industry, such as energy, technology, health, or financial. You can usually recognize a sector fund because the industry it focuses on will be in the name of the fund, such as ABC Technology Fund.

Since sector funds do focus on one particular industry, they are usually very volatile. When the industry involved is doing well, the value of the fund will rise dramatically, but it will also fall just as dramatically if the industry is on a downward spiral.

Many mutual fund holders who use sector funds trade them frequently as they jump from industry to industry, hoping to pick the industry that will be on top each year. While this type of frequent trading can result in large gains, these gains can be wiped out or significantly reduced by fees charged for selling mutual fund shares too quickly. To discourage this type of trading, many mutual funds charge a fee of 1 to 2 percent of your holdings if you exit the fund in less than a year. Don't use mutual funds if you truly want to trade in and out of industries frequently; other types of stock-trading vehicles will better meet your needs.

International

You also may want to invest internationally. Often when the U.S. stock market is down, you can find a market somewhere else in the world that is doing well. International fund managers focus on buying stocks on foreign exchanges.

There are two types of international funds—world (or global) funds and foreign funds. World fund managers will buy U.S. stocks as well as stocks on foreign exchanges. They try to pick the stocks for their portfolios by focusing on companies in countries that have the best chance of appreciation in a given year. For example, if European stocks are

expected to see the next growth spurt, they'll buy
stocks primarily in European companies.

Foreign fund managers also seek growth by picking
stocks from companies in countries whose markets are expected to do the best economically. The
major difference is that foreign fund managers will
not hold any stock from U.S. companies. They buy
only foreign stocks.

Mutual Aids

> Investing only in this country is far too
> limiting. Stock markets in different parts
> of the world tend to hit their peaks and
> valleys at different times because of vary-
> ing economic conditions. By diversifying
> your mutual fund portfolio with international
> funds, you can keep your portfolio on a
> steadier growth path.

Truthfully, if your primary goal is to add an international component to your personal portfolio, you're
better off with a foreign fund. Otherwise you could
end up with considerable overlap between your
world fund choice and your growth fund choice.

Bond

Bond or fixed-income funds invest primarily in
bonds and preferred stocks. Bonds are essentially
a type of loan. A company or the government sells

bonds to borrow cash. A bondholder, in exchange for lending the bond issuer cash, gets paid interest on this loan.

Your bond fund earnings can be either taxable or tax-free.

- Taxable fixed-income funds hold corporate and long-term federal government bonds.
- Tax-free fixed funds hold municipal bonds, which are bonds issued by states and local governments. Tax-free bond funds are free from taxes on interest earned but can be taxed on capital gains.

Many people look to bonds for safety, especially with a market as volatile as we have seen in recent years. Others seek bonds for current income.

While bond funds offer better income than a money market fund, there is still risk to your principal that you do not face with a money market fund. Bonds can lose face value. The face value of a bond is the amount of money you will get when the bond comes due (or matures). That's when the bond issuer must repay the bondholder the money they borrowed.

The value of a bond can go up or down when interest rates change. When interest rates go up, the value of a bond goes down. For example, if you hold a bond that pays 4 percent interest and newly issued bonds are paying 5 percent interest, your 4 percent bond would not be as attractive to a buyer. A person who wants to buy a bond would prefer the one that pays higher interest. So if you need to sell your bond, which is only paying 4 percent interest, you have to sell that bond at less than its face value to make it more attractive to the buyer.

Stability in fixed-income funds varies by what the fund manager selects as investments. Consider three things when purchasing a bond fund:

- Type of bonds in the portfolio
- Credit quality of the bonds
- Average maturity (when the bondholder will get back the value of the bond from the company or government that borrowed the money)

The U.S. Treasury, a U.S. government agency, corporations, and state and local municipal governments issue bonds.

Remember bonds are debt instruments. The issuer sells bonds to generate cash for a certain time period. In exchange for borrowing this cash, the issuer pays interest over a set period of years. The creditworthiness of the issuer is, of course, critical to a bond's principal security. The safest are those issued by the U.S. Treasury or a U.S. government agency. Moody's and Standard & Poor's are bond-rating agencies that can help you determine the investment quality of bonds.

Investment-grade bonds receive Aaa or AAA ratings to Baa or BBB ratings from Moody's or S&P. Speculative or junk bonds' ratings vary from Ba or BB to D. The lower the rating the higher the yield, as well as the greater the risk. Bond funds that offer higher yields are usually investing in speculative bonds, so be sure you understand the risks of the funds you select.

Average maturity is also a factor in bond return. Short-term bonds have an average life of 1 to 5 years. Intermediate-term bonds mature in 5 to 10 years. Long-term bonds have a life span over 10 years. Bond funds also are generally grouped by these maturity factors.

> **Mutual Aids**
>
> You don't stand to make as much money with a bond fund as you would with a successful growth fund, but you also don't risk losing as much principal in a bad year.

Money Market

Money market funds invest in short-term debt securities (vehicles used to borrow money) of the U.S. Government, banks, and corporations, as well as U.S. Treasury Bills. These funds offer the highest stability of principal of any mutual fund while at the same time seeking moderate to high current income. They have no potential for capital appreciation.

Safety is the primary reason people choose money market funds. Investors can usually depend on a constant share price of $1. Any volatility is reflected in the current yield (the percentage by which your holdings will increase in value) or interest rate.

Money market funds can be an attractive alternative to bank accounts because their yields are usually somewhat higher than savings accounts, but lower than certificates of deposit (CDs).

The greatest advantage money market funds have over CDs is their accessibility. You can withdraw money at any time without penalty. Money market funds also offer check-writing privileges. Some money market funds do limit the number of free checks per month and will charge a fee once you exceed that limit.

Money market funds are not insured by the *Federal Deposit Insurance Company (FDIC)*, but invest only in highly liquid, short-term, top-rated money market instruments. These funds are good if you need high stability of principal and can live with moderate current income. Your cash will be readily available when you need it.

def•i•ni•tion

The **Federal Deposit Insurance Company (FDIC)** protects the first $100,000 of deposits in most banks. Be sure your bank displays the FDIC symbol and indicates your checking and savings accounts are protected.

There are three types of money market funds to consider:

- General money market funds
- Funds that invest only in U.S. Government bills, notes, and bonds
- Tax-exempt money market funds

General money market funds invest in a combination of all types of short-term debt securities. If you want a fund that is safer, choose one that only buys U.S. government debt securities, whose principal and interest is backed by the U.S. government or its agencies. The cost of this guarantee is slightly lower interest rates than general money market funds.

Mutual Aids

Money market funds are suitable for you if you are seeking high stability of principal and moderate current income with immediate liquidity. They are also a good place to park your money until you have time to research the best investment for it, because you can't lose the principal value of your portfolio.

Tax-exempt money market funds invest in short-term, high-rated municipal obligations that are exempt from federal and possibly state and local income taxes. Generally their yields offer the lowest return among money market mutual funds, so compare the after-tax yields for both taxable and nontaxable money market funds to determine which is best for you.

Balanced

Balanced mutual funds, also known as Asset Allocation or Hybrid funds, represent the smallest piece of the mutual fund pie. Only about 6.5 percent of the 8,000 mutual funds on the market fit into this category. These funds invest in a combination of stocks, bonds, and cash reserves. Balanced mutual fund managers seek to provide:

- High level of current income from dividends and interest
- Long-term capital growth
- Low risk to the value of the portfolio

Well-managed balanced funds are usually the least volatile of all the funds that include stocks and bonds. The goal of these funds is not to achieve the highest possible return but to generate income and growth with an acceptable level of risk.

You will never find a balanced fund in a top 10 mutual fund list. The flip side of this coin is that unless you have selected an incompetent manager, you will never find one in the bottom 10 either.

The inclusion of bonds for current income and significant cash reserves to minimize risk will lower the growth opportunity in exchange for a safer investment. In some balanced funds, the manager is required to maintain a certain mix, for example 60 percent stocks and 40 percent bonds. Others have stated objectives that give their managers more leeway.

Mutual Aids

Balanced funds invest in both the stock and bond markets. This makes their returns less volatile. Your portfolio will not grow as quickly with balanced funds, but you may sleep better at night because you don't have to worry as much about losing your principal.

Life-Cycle

A new type of fund now available on the market is the life-cycle fund. This is the closest thing to putting your mutual fund portfolio on automatic pilot and letting someone else worry about it. That someone else is usually a *mutual fund family*.

def•i•ni•tion

A **mutual fund family** is a group of funds managed under the same company umbrella. Some well-known families include Vanguard, Fidelity, and T. Rowe Price.

Life-cycle funds, called "age-based funds" or "target-date funds," are a unique breed of balanced funds. While they do include stocks, bonds, and cash, their asset allocation shifts based on your growth needs at a specific age.

Initially the portfolio will be more growth oriented, but as you get closer to retirement, the asset allocation is automatically adjusted to become more conservative.

For example, Vanguard offers the Target Retirement series. One of the funds in this series is called the Target Retirement 2025 Fund, which is designed to build a portfolio appropriately for people who plan to retire within five years of 2025.

These types of funds are great for people who don't have the time or the knowledge to manage a mutual fund portfolio to reach their goals for retirement. Professional managers help you keep your mix of investments on track to meet your goals.

 Fund Fears

If you choose to invest using life-cycle funds, look very closely at the fees you will pay. Their fees often are twice the amount you would pay for management compared to the fees you would pay if you pick the individual funds yourself.

While these types of funds can be a good idea, if you are clueless about how to build a portfolio, watch your fees closely. You actually pay fees to two types of managers when you use life-cycle funds. You pay a fee to the manager who chooses the mutual funds to keep the proper age-based allocation. You also pay a fee to the managers who manage the individual mutual fund portfolios that are chosen for the life-cycle fund.

The Least You Need to Know

- Stock mutual funds offer the greatest potential for gains, but also are the riskiest.
- Bond mutual funds generate more income than an interest-bearing bank account, but you do risk the possibility of losing principal.
- Money market funds are the safest investment but offer the lowest returns.
- Balanced or life-cycle funds combine all three—stock funds, bond funds, and money market funds—to develop a well-balanced portfolio for you.

How to Invest in Mutual Funds

In This Chapter

- Getting funds through your workplace
- The use of a professional
- Doing it yourself
- Read the fine print

You may already own mutual funds and not even know it. If you have a retirement savings plan at work, such as a 401(k), you probably have some mutual funds offered as investment alternatives.

In addition to your workplace, you can buy mutual funds from many different sources, such as through banks, insurance companies, brokerage firms, or directly from mutual fund companies.

In this chapter, we review these various sources and discuss the key documents you should review before buying a fund.

Buying Funds at Work

Many people buy their mutual funds through their employer-based retirement savings accounts, such as 401(k)s or 403(b)s. While this can be a great way to save, especially if your employer matches your contributions, you don't have very many mutual funds from which to choose because the company usually designates only 10 to 15 funds from which you must make your choices.

Buying mutual funds through your workplace is definitely the easiest way to do it, though. Your company gives you a form to fill out and then buys the mutual funds for your retirement savings portfolio based on the choices you indicate on that form. They automatically take money out of your paycheck each pay period and deposit it in the retirement savings account. It's easy and painless once you fill out the form.

The form is usually one of many forms you fill out when you are first hired. Your company's rules for retirement benefits can be set up in such a way that you don't qualify until you've been employed for 12 months. If that's the case, you may not get the form until your first anniversary on the job. In addition to the form, you'll receive a package of information about each of the investment alternatives, which can include company stock, mutual funds, and traditional fixed-rate savings accounts.

Carefully review the information about each of the investment options before you make your choices.

In addition to the list of investment choices, the company should give you information about each option's performance. For mutual funds, this should include performance information over the past year, the past 5 years, the past 10 years (if available), and for the lifetime of the fund. You should also find information about each mutual fund's management team and its experience in managing funds.

Fund Facts

For many investors, their first exposure to mutual funds is through employer-sponsored retirement savings. In fact, almost 60 percent of mutual fund shareholders purchased their first mutual fund in this way. In 2005, about 32 percent of mutual fund shareholders held their funds inside employer-sponsored retirement savings plans only, 31 percent held mutual funds inside employer-sponsored savings plans plus held mutual funds outside those plans, and 37 percent held all their mutual funds outside employer-sponsored plans.

Sometimes the investment company that manages the employer-sponsored retirement accounts designs and manages the mutual fund options, so you won't be able to research the funds through a third-party source. But many times you will find that the list of mutual funds being offered includes publicly traded mutual funds you can purchase on the open market.

You can independently research any publicly traded mutual funds. We show you how to do that in Chapter 5, where we explore how to research funds and make the right choices.

Seeking Advice from Professionals

More than 80 percent of mutual fund shareholders seek professional advice before buying their funds. About 50 percent of mutual fund shareholders only buy mutual funds through professional advisors, while about 30 percent seek the advice of professionals but also buy funds on their own.

Many people lack sufficient knowledge about how to invest wisely, so they seek the advice of professionals before buying their mutual funds. If you don't know much about investing, a professional advisor is a good choice to help get you started. But as you invest through a professional advisor to build your portfolio, take the time to research and learn more yourself.

Your portfolio will grow a lot faster if commissions and fees don't eat it up as you invest. We talk more about how to invest in mutual funds on your own in the following section "Going It Alone."

You can seek the help of professionals in many different ways. Professional advisors can include full-service brokers, independent financial planners, banks and savings institutions, insurance agents, and accountants. In most cases these professionals will place the mutual fund buy and sell orders for you.

Full-Service Brokers

However, a full-service broker does much more than just buy and sell mutual funds for you. His services also include research, investment advice, tax tips, and estate planning. You do pay a price for these services, though—commissions can range from 3 percent to 8.5 percent.

Each time you put money into a mutual fund purchased through the broker, he takes out these commissions. For example, if you plan to invest $1,000 in mutual funds and you do so through a broker that charges a 6 percent commission (known as a load), the broker takes his commission up front. So $60 goes to the broker and $940 goes into the fund.

Brokers also tend to push the "house brands." For example, if you work with a broker from Merrill Lynch or American Express, your broker will likely recommend his company's mutual funds because he makes higher commissions if he sells them. If you truly want independent advice about which mutual funds to choose, don't depend upon a full-service broker.

Independent Financial Planners

Independent financial planners not directly affiliated with a brokerage firm or insurance company will more likely be a good source of advice that is not tainted by the company the advisor works for or by the commissions the advisor will make.

In fact, if you seek out an experienced independent financial advisor who is *fee-based*, you won't have to worry about his mutual fund recommendations being tainted by commissions he will make. Before you start to work with a financial planner, be sure you know how that planner will be compensated. You don't want a planner who recommends a mutual fund solely because he will make more money on his commissions.

def•i•ni•tion

Fee-based financial advisors charge set fees based on the work you ask them to do. Their fee can be based on an hourly charge or on a percentage of the assets you want them to manage.

Before a financial planner will advise you on which mutual funds you should pick, he will first assess your financial health by looking at your assets, your debt, and your current and future financial needs. He then will make any investment recommendations based on your short- and long-term financial goals.

The best way to find an independent financial advisor is through recommendations from a friend or family member. If you don't know anyone who can recommend a good financial advisor, you can locate one near you through the Financial Planning Association (www.fpanet.org/public). At their website you'll find articles about how to select a financial advisor, as well as a database you can search to find an advisor who will best meet your needs.

Even after you get the advice of a financial planner, you will most likely have to make arrangements to buy the mutual funds recommended through another source. Your best bet is to buy the funds either directly from the mutual fund company or through a discount broker or mutual fund supermarket. We talk more about those options below.

Banks and Savings Institutions

Many banks and savings institutions provide financial advisors through whom you can purchase mutual funds as well as other investment vehicles, such as stocks. You will have to pay commissions, which can be as high as those you'll find at a full-service broker, so find out how much you'll pay in fees or commissions before starting to work with someone at your bank.

Many banks and savings institutions have their own mutual funds or have an arrangement with a specific mutual fund family. The fees and commissions are higher when you choose a mutual fund from the in-house *mutual fund family*. While the up-front commission or load may be lower than what you might find with a full-service broker, you may find that the yearly fees are higher. We talk more about commissions, fees, and hidden costs in Chapter 4.

def•i•ni•tion

> A **mutual fund family** is a group of mutual funds under one company umbrella. Two of the best-known mutual fund families are Fidelity and Vanguard.

If you do decide to work with your bank or other financial institution, be sure you understand the commissions and fees you will pay. Compare that fee structure to one you would get investing directly with a mutual fund company.

Insurance Agents

Many times insurance agents will use the title of financial planner, but you won't truly be getting independent advice. Financial planners tied to an insurance company are not truly independent but will tend to recommend the mutual funds for which they will get the best commissions.

These commissions are not only based on the commission or load you pay up front, but you will also find hidden charges included in the annual costs paid for holding the mutual funds. We review those costs in Chapter 4.

Some mutual funds purchased through insurance agents or brokers also have back-end commissions or loads. These loads are charged when you sell your fund and can result in an even greater loss than a load paid when you buy a fund that is front-loaded (fees paid when purchased). Fees based on the amount of money you take out of a fund when it is sold can actually be higher. That's because at the time you sell a fund, you'll pay fees not only on what you spent to buy the fund but also on any gains you earned while you held the fund.

Accountants

Your accountant can be a good source of investment information and is more likely to charge you
based on a fee rather than being reimbursed by the
mutual fund company. Most accountants do not get
involved in the buying and selling of mutual funds
and do not earn a commission on the recommendations they make.

Some Certified Public Accountants (CPAs) seek
additional certification as financial planners. You
can find out more about this additional certification
and find CPA Financial Planners near you with the
certification at pfp.aicpa.org.

Myths You'll Hear About Load Funds

When you start talking with professional advisors,
many of them will tout the advantages of buying
load funds. These advantages are myths. Don't
believe them. Study after study has clearly shown
there is no specific advantage to buying mutual
funds with a load (where a commission is paid) versus a no-load (where no commission in paid). You
may want a professional advisor to help you sort out
your investment choices, but don't seek professional
help when all you need is assistance for actually
doing the transaction.

You'll likely hear these myths about load funds:

- "You don't pay my commission, I'm paid by
  the mutual fund company." Technically it
  might be true that the person selling you the

fund receives his check from the mutual fund company, but you are the one paying that commission. The commission a salesperson receives can be based on a front load (a percentage paid when you first buy the fund), a back load (a percentage paid when you sell the fund) or a hidden fee (a percentage paid yearly to cover marketing costs, called a 12b-1 fee). We talk more about these fees and the impact they have on your mutual fund earnings in Chapter 4.

- "Load funds have better fund managers." There is no truth to this myth. You can find good and bad managers in both load and no-load funds. Just because a fund has a load does not impact how good the manager will be. The manager does not make any money on the fund's load. That all goes to the selling broker.

- "No-load funds have higher fees." The opposite is actually true. You will usually find that no-load fund fees are lower year to year than funds with loads.

- "You'll have a hard time getting through to a no-load company on a busy day. I can give you better service." Don't believe it. In fact, a broker is just one person and can be out on appointments or taking other calls just when you need to talk with him. A no-load mutual fund family from which you buy directly will have a bank of people who can assist. Some even have customer service people available 24 hours a day.

- "You won't get advice on when is the best time to buy and sell funds." Mutual funds are not an investment that you should buy and sell frequently. Unless a major shift in a fund's investment objective or management occurs, you really don't have a reason to want to sell a fund as long as you've done your homework in picking good funds. Brokers make their money by encouraging the buying and selling of investments, but you don't. When you buy and sell load funds, you pay commissions just to complete the transaction.

Going It Alone

Even if you initially start buying mutual funds with the help of a professional financial advisor, we recommend you gradually wean yourself off of that help and make your own buying and selling decisions. While periodically checking your goals and financial health with an independent financial advisor is a good thing, you don't need to pay the costs of an advisor managing your mutual fund choices on top of the costs you pay for a professionally managed mutual fund. You get the help of a professional money manager just by buying the mutual fund.

Your cheapest way to buy mutual funds is directly from the no-load mutual fund company. You won't pay any transaction fees when you buy directly from a mutual fund company. But you may like the convenience of buying mutual funds through a fund supermarket. Let's take a look at these two options.

Buying Directly Through Mutual Fund Companies

You can buy your mutual funds at the lowest cost by buying them directly through no-load (no commission) mutual fund companies. Few no-load mutual fund families are out there, but here are seven top no-load mutual fund companies in alphabetical order with their web addresses to help you locate them more easily:

- Dodge & Cox Funds (www.dodgeandcox.com) or call 1-800-621-3979
- Fidelity (www.fidelity.com) or call 1-800-544-9797
- Janus (www.janus.com) or call 1-800-525-0020
- Oakmark (www.oakmark.com) or call 1-800-625-6275
- TIAA-CREF (www.tiaa-cref.org/products/mutual) or call 1-800-223-1200
- T. Rowe Price (www.troweprice.com) or call 1-800-638-5660
- Vanguard (www.vanguard.com) or call 1-800-997-2798

You can buy and sell funds from any of these no-load companies by contacting the company directly. You can do transactions by telephone, mail, or electronically. They all offer ways to invest and manage your accounts online.

You can download an application form as well as the prospectus for each mutual fund that interests you from their website, or you can call and ask them to send it to you. Always read a mutual fund's prospectus before investing in the fund.

As you sort through the information and have questions about the process of opening an account, selling funds, or getting more detail about a fund's portfolio or its investment objectives, call the fund and speak with one of their telephone advisors.

You will find the people handling their phone banks very knowledgeable about the mutual fund company's products and which of their funds might be good for you to consider given your personal investment objectives. While they can't specifically help you make investment decisions, they can help lead you through the maze of information available.

Fund Facts

The application you need to fill out for a mutual fund is similar to any application you've completed for most financial institutions. You'll give your contact information, employer, citizenship, the type of account you want to set up (such as joint account, custodial account, IRA account), and driver's license. You will also designate how you will fund your account (by check, electronic transfer, wire, or transfer from another financial institution, such as another mutual fund company).

When you are ready to buy a mutual fund from one of these companies, fill out the application form, which you can do manually and mail to the mutual fund company or complete online.

Then specify which mutual fund or funds you want to purchase and how much you plan to deposit in each fund. For example, suppose you have $3,000 to invest in Fidelity funds, and you want to put $1,000 in each of three Fidelity funds, so list the fund names and the amount you want to buy next to each fund name.

Next you'll be asked how you want to handle withdrawals from your funds. You can arrange to have any withdrawals electronically deposited in your bank account. You also can arrange for funds to be transferred by telephone instructions. Or you can designate that your funds can only be withdrawn by written instructions sent to the mutual fund company by mail.

You also have the option of opening a money market account with the mutual fund company and having the money from any mutual fund sales deposited in that account until you decide what you want to do with the money. Most of these money market accounts can be set up with check-writing privileges that you can use as you would use any other bank checking account.

Sometimes these money market accounts have a minimum dollar amount for any checks you write. For example, the fund company may specify that the minimum amount for which you can write a check is $100 or $500. If there are limits on the dollar amount of checks or number of checks you can write per month, you're probably better off depositing the money in your regular checking account and using your regular banking account for smaller checks you may want to write.

Using Mutual Fund Supermarkets

Mutual fund supermarkets continue to build in popularity. No, these are not like a food store where you can walk in and pick one fund down aisle one and a second down aisle two. Instead they are like an online mutual fund marketplace where you can choose funds offered by many different fund companies.

Their big advantage is convenience. You can open an account with one mutual fund supermarket and buy funds from many different companies rather than have accounts at each mutual fund company that has a fund you want to own. You also get only one statement that has all your investments and their performance listed, rather than having to sort through statements from each mutual fund company and trying to piece together your portfolio's performance. The disadvantage is that you will pay for these conveniences.

Each mutual fund supermarket has its own fee structure. You will usually find that some of the mutual funds on the list have lower fees or commissions to buy than others because the mutual fund supermarket has a sales or marketing agreement with that company. Watch your fees closely, and be sure you can get the mutual funds you want without having to pay a sizeable commission or fee.

You will find mutual fund supermarkets offered by both brokers and large mutual fund companies. Three top brokers that offer mutual fund supermarkets are:

- Charles Schwab (www.schwab.com) Schwab developed the first mutual fund supermarket. To find its mutual fund supermarket, which is called "OneSource," click on the "Investment Products" tab, then on the "Mutual Funds" tab.

- E-Trade (us.etrade.com/e/t/invest/mfgettingstarted)

- TD Waterhouse (www.tdameritrade.com/researchideas/mutualfundsetfs/fundFamilies.html)

Two large no-load mutual fund companies that provide their customers with the ability to buy funds, or even stocks, through their supermarkets include:

- Vanguard (www.vanguard.com) To find the mutual fund supermarket, when you get to the website click on "Go to the site." Then click on the link to "Brokerage services for investing in stocks, bonds, and non-Vanguard funds."

- Fidelity (www.fidelity.com) Fidelity calls its supermarket the FundsNetwork. You can find it by clicking on the link to "Mutual Funds" in the column on the left side of the page called "Our Products." On the mutual fund page you will see the link "Explore more than 4,500 funds."

Only those inside the mutual fund supermarkets really know exactly what listing on these mutual fund supermarkets cost the mutual fund companies. At this point, there is no requirement for the mutual fund supermarkets to publicly state what they charge mutual funds as listing fees or what other money may exchange hands between the mutual fund and the supermarket. The mutual fund supermarkets negotiate various types of marketing arrangements, which can help to position the mutual funds better on the "shelf." What I mean by "shelf" in this virtual world is the placement on the website and the visibility of the funds being offered. Better "shelf" space means more visible placement for the fund.

 Fund Fears

If you choose to purchase funds through mutual fund supermarkets, don't just pick the funds whose positions are the most visible. That does not necessarily mean that the fund is a "best pick"; it just means that the mutual fund company paid more money for better placement. Always do your own research before picking a mutual fund.

You will find mutual funds listed at the mutual fund supermarket grouped into four categories:

- **House Brands**—These are the brands the mutual fund supermarket wants you to buy. Obviously, if you are buying through

Fidelity, its house brand is Fidelity Mutual Funds.

- **No Transaction Fee Funds**—These are funds you can buy through the supermarket without paying any additional fees. You probably will have some fees that you pay just for opening an account with a mutual fund supermarket, but these fees will disappear as your account grows above $100,000. The mutual fund supermarket in these cases has some type of marketing agreement with each mutual fund company, which you may pay for through hidden fees, such as 12b-1 fees, which I explain in Chapter 4.

- **Transaction Fee Funds**—These are funds you will pay a transaction fee to buy through the supermarket. The fees vary depending on the type of fund and the agreement the supermarket has with the fund family. Sometimes you will find you can buy the fund much cheaper by going directly to the mutual fund company, just because the mutual fund supermarket wants to promote its own brand. For example, if you open an account at Fidelity and want to buy a Vanguard mutual fund, you will pay a fee even though the Vanguard funds are no-load.

Applications to open an account with one of the mutual fund supermarkets are very similar to the application you would fill out for a direct account with a mutual fund company or financial institution.

You can complete this application online, by telephone, or by mail.

Exploring Fund Documents

Before buying any mutual fund, always read the prospectus for the fund as well as any account agreement. In that prospectus you will find the investment objectives and policies, the fund expenses, investment risks, performance records, and account management information.

Investment Objectives and Policies

You will usually find the fund's objectives and policies on the front page of the prospectus. For example, a fund that invests conservatively might say that its objectives are to "conserve principal" but looks to "attain a reasonable income return without undue risk." A fund whose objective is growth may state that "the fund seeks to invest in growth-oriented stocks, which may entail considerable risk to principal."

The policies included in this section should include the types of investments the fund can choose, such as stocks, bonds, foreign securities, options, or futures. You will also see a breakdown on the percentage of the portfolio that can be held in each type of investment, such as 50 percent of the portfolio will be held in bonds, 40 percent will be held in stocks, and 10 percent with be held in cash or cash equivalents.

Fund Expenses

You should see a clear description of fund expenses and fees you will pay as a shareholder in the fund. If there are any sales loads (commissions) to be paid, this should be listed. This will include not only the commission paid up front, but also commissions you may have to pay on any dividends reinvested. You also may have to pay fees to sell the fund or exchange the fund to a different fund in the same fund family. All these loads and fees should be listed.

In addition to sales fees, you will see a listing of operating expenses that include management expenses, investment advisor fees, shareholder accounting costs, 12b-1 fees, distribution costs, and other expenses. We delve more deeply into these fees and what they mean in Chapter 4.

Investment Risks

You should also see a statement that discusses the risks entailed in investing through this mutual fund. For example, if you are investing in a mutual fund that buys stocks as part of its portfolio, you will see a warning to indicate that a general stock decline will impact negatively upon the value of the mutual fund.

We talk more about the types of investment risks in Chapter 1.

Performance Record

You should find a record of the fund's performance throughout its lifetime in the fund's prospectus, as

well as performance results for the past year, the
past 5 years, and the past 10 years.

Mutual fund investment usually is for the long haul,
so be concerned primarily with long-term performance. While the one-year return may look very
good for a fund that invested in technology stocks
in the year 1999 before the crash, that same fund in
2001 will look like a disaster. It likely dropped 30 to
40 percent or more in value.

In addition to the mutual fund's own performance
history, you should also find the performance history for an index of similar types of investment
vehicles. For example, if you are buying a bond
fund, you should see a comparison to a bond
index. That way you can compare the mutual fund
management's success in matching or beating the
market over various periods of time.

Account Management Information

You should find information about how to open an
account and how to invest additional money into
the mutual fund after initially purchasing the fund.

Most funds offer automatic reinvestment of both
the dividends and capital gains. You should sign up
for this service unless you need the mutual fund as
a current income source. Your portfolio will grow
much faster if you automatically reinvest any money
made on the investment.

If you do want to take out some funds and reinvest
others, you will find a cash dividend option, which

pays you all dividend income but reinvests all capital gains. You can choose an all cash option where you will be paid all dividends and capital gains.

You will also find information about how to withdraw funds and the signature guarantees that will be required. You will find policies on transaction cancellation, which usually is not possible once you have completed a transaction.

In addition, you will find information on when you can complete a trade. For example, most funds close transactions as of 4 P.M. each trading day. If your instructions for a trade are received after that time, the trade won't be completed until the next trading day. Mutual funds trade on any day that the banks are open. You cannot trade mutual funds on bank holidays or weekends.

Other information in the prospectus includes how to exchange your fund for another fund in the same family. If you are opening an account with a mutual fund supermarket, you will get information on how to exchange funds for other funds in the supermarket. You should also find information about any services offered by the mutual fund company, such as telephone transfers, electronic transfers, or wire services.

In the next chapter, we focus on the one thing that can be the biggest drag on your investment portfolio—loads and fees.

The Least You Need to Know

- You can buy mutual funds directly through the mutual fund company, or you can purchase them through a professional advisor, such as a broker, banker, or insurance agent.

- Mutual funds for which you must pay a commission (load) do not get better returns than no-load funds. Whether or not you pay a load is not a significant indicator of a good or bad fund.

- Always carefully read the fine print of a mutual fund prospectus before you invest in the fund.

Chapter 4

Commissions and Fees Can Be a Drag

In This Chapter

- Paying commissions
- Fueling fees
- Ruining returns

Everyone who invests by using mutual funds must pay to have his funds managed professionally. That's what you pay for when you seek a money manager and what you want when you choose to invest using mutual funds.

The key is finding alternatives that will minimize those costs, so more of your money can be put to work for you. To minimize those costs, you need to learn the basics of managing a mutual fund portfolio, but once you've made your initial fund choices, your portfolio can run on autopilot with only a few minor adjustments a couple of times per year. So why pay a salesperson to pick your funds for you?

In this chapter, we dig into the truth about mutual fund commission structures and ongoing operating fees. We help you understand what you are paying for when you buy a fund. You will find all fees and charges for a fund spelled out near the front of the fund's prospectus, under the heading "Shareholder Fees."

Sorting Out Commissions

You will have to pay commissions called sales charges or loads when you purchase a mutual fund through a broker, insurance agent, or representative from another type of financial institution. The only time you don't have to pay a commission is when you buy a mutual fund that is sold by a company that does not charge a load—known as no-load mutual funds.

The most common type of load is a front-end load, but there are also back-end loads, most often called deferred sales charges. These loads are like sales commissions and are paid to the person (or his company) that sells you the fund.

In addition to loads, you can have purchase fees, redemption fees, exchange fees, and account fees. In this section, we sort out sales charges and sales fees to help you understand what you pay to buy, sell, or exchange a load mutual fund.

Sales Charge (Load) on Purchases

When you buy a mutual fund and pay a percentage load or sales charge, this is known as a "front-end load." In most cases this fee goes to the brokerage company that sells you the fund. The big difference with mutual funds is that you as the buyer pay the commission rather than the person selling the product—the mutual fund company.

It's sort of like what happens in real estate when you work with a buyer's agent who helps you find the right home. In most real estate transactions, the seller pays the real estate commission, but in some transactions the buyer pays the commission if he specifically hired the buyer's agent to find his home.

When you pay a front-end load, the percentage amount of the load reduces your investment. For example, suppose you want to buy $1,000 worth of shares in a mutual fund that is sold with a 5.75 percent front-end load. The $57.75 sales load you pay is subtracted from the amount that goes into the mutual fund. When you get your first state-ment, you'll see that only $942.25 was invested in the fund.

Mutual fund loads usually range between 3 percent and 8.5 percent. They can't be any higher than 8.5 percent because that is the maximum set by the *National Association of Securities Dealers (NASD)*, the primary regulatory agency for the sale of mutual funds.

Deferred Sales Charge (Load)

Not all sales charges or loads are paid up front. Sometimes you'll see the words "deferred sales charge." You pay these charges, also referred to as a "back-end" sales load, when you sell the fund.

def•i•ni•tion

National Association of Securities Dealers (**NASD**) is the primary private-sector regulator of the U.S. securities industry. NASD regulates the activities of more than 5,100 brokerage firms and more than 659,800 registered securities representatives. Anyone who sells you mutual funds should be registered with the NASD.

When you purchase mutual fund shares that are subject to a back-end sales load rather than a front-end sales load, your full initial investment is deposited into the fund to buy shares. Often these back-end loads are like hidden fees because the mutual fund purchaser may not be fully aware that he will pay a commission when he sells the fund.

If you are buying a mutual fund with a deferred sales charge or back-end load, carefully read the fine print for how that load will be calculated. The load can be calculated based on your initial investment or based on your redemption amount (the amount you receive when you sell the fund). The most common wording is that the mutual fund will calculate your back-end load based on the lesser value either of your initial investment or your redemption amount.

That way if the fund gains money, you only pay the load based on your initial investment. For example, suppose you invest $1,000, and it increases to $1,500 in two years. Your back-end load was 5 percent. The lesser amount to calculate this 5 percent back-end load on would be $1,000, so you would pay $50 for your back-end load.

Now, let's reverse that and consider a situation where your back-end load mutual fund loses value and drops from your $1,000 initial investment to just $850 in two years. When you sell the fund, you'll pay your back-end load based on the lower amount of $850, or $42.50.

Some funds base the deferred sales charge solely on the redemption amount, which means if the fund gains in value, you will pay a higher deferred sales charge than you would if the load were a front-end load. For example, suppose you invest $1,000 in the fund and it goes up in value to $1,500 when you decide to sell it in two years. If your deferred sales charge or back-end load is 5 percent, you will pay $75.

Fund Fears

Carefully read and understand how your deferred sales charge or back-end load will be calculated. The most equitable arrangement is for you to pay the lesser of two possible calculations—one based on the initial investment and the second based on the redemption amount.

You will find that the most common type of back-end sales load is the "contingent deferred sales load," also referred to as a "CDSC" or "CDSL." When this type of back load is used, the amount of load you pay will depend on how long you hold on to the fund. In fact, you could end up paying no load at all if you hold on to the fund for the required number of years for the load to change to zero.

For example, suppose you buy a fund with a 5 percent back-end load with a CDSL. If you sell that fund during the first year, you will pay a 5 percent back-end load based on the initial investment. If you hold that fund for more than one year, but less than two years, you will pay 4 percent on the initial investment. If you hold the fund for more than two years, but less than three years, you will pay 3 percent on the initial investment. That amount would continue to drop each year held until it reaches zero.

 Mutual Aids

> If you do want to sell a back-end load mutual fund with a CDSC or CDSL load, be sure you know when your change to a lower load percentage takes place. You may find that if you hold the fund for just a few more weeks, you'll pay 1 percent less in fees.

You will also find an additional marketing fee, called a 12b-1 fee, in most funds that have loads. That fee, which we explain later in this chapter, covers the marketing expenses of the mutual fund. It's paid to the mutual fund administrator rather than the salesperson.

Purchase Fee

Some mutual funds charge a purchase fee to their shareholders when they buy shares of the fund. This fee is paid to the mutual fund company and not to the broker or mutual fund supermarket that initiated the sale.

The purchase fee covers the fund's costs associated with the purchase. Look for purchase fees when buying a mutual fund from any source other than the mutual fund company managing the fund.

Redemption Fee

Some mutual funds charge a redemption fee to shareholders when they sell their shares. This fee is usually a percentage deducted from the redemption proceeds, but it's not a sales load.

The funds collected are generally used to cover the costs associated with handling a shareholder's redemption and are paid directly to the fund, not to a broker. Redemption fees are usually 1 or 2 percent. The maximum a fund can charge is 2 percent, which is a limit set by the U.S. Securities and Exchange Commission.

Before you buy a fund, find out if there is a redemption fee and what the rules are surrounding that fee. Most times a mutual fund will set that fee to discourage mutual fund traders, who hold shares of a mutual fund for a very short time, such as less than 60 to 90 days. Sometimes you'll see redemption fees charged for shares sold before holding them for a year.

When a person sells a mutual fund, the mutual fund company must by law have the funds available for the redemption, which can mean that the mutual fund company will have to sell shares of stock if they don't have enough cash on hand. That can result in additional costs to the mutual fund shareholders who continue to hold the fund. The redemption fee reimburses at least part of those costs.

Exchange Fee

Some mutual fund families charge a fee if you want to exchange your mutual fund holdings for another fund in the same fund family. Check your fund's prospectus for details about how to exchange funds. You may also find some information on exchange fees in your fund's purchase agreement. If you can't find any mention of exchange fees, ask about them before you buy the fund, so you aren't hit with any surprises after you've already purchased the fund.

Account Fee

Some mutual fund families charge a small fee, such as $10, for each account you open to pay for the yearly maintenance of your account. In most cases this fee is waived once the value of your account reaches above a certain dollar amount, such as $10,000. Don't forget to ask if there is a yearly account maintenance fee before opening an account.

Going to Class

If you buy mutual funds with front- or back-end loads, you will also likely find out that these funds are in classes, and we're not talking about the kind you attend when you go to school. Many mutual fund companies offer their load funds in more than one class of shares.

For example, you may see a fund that offers "Class A" and "Class B" shares. Each class will invest in the same portfolio of stocks and bonds, and each will have the same investment objectives and policies. The key differences will be based on the shareholder services and/or distribution arrangements, especially related to the fees and expenses you'll pay. So each class will likely have different performance results depending on how much of the earnings are taken out in fees. We talk more about the drag on earnings in the section titled "How Commissions and Fees Impact Your Returns."

Here are some key characteristics of the most common mutual fund share classes offered to individual investors:

- **Class A Shares** Class A shares typically are front-end load funds. Because you pay the commissions up front, you will usually find that their fees and annual expenses are lower than other load mutual fund share classes.

- **Class B Shares** Class B shares typically are back-end load funds. These types of shares will usually have a contingent deferred sales load, as well as higher annual fees and expenses than Class A shares.

- **Class C Shares**   Class C shares can have either a front-end load, a back-end load, or possibly some combination of the two. Class C Shares will have higher fees and annual expenses than Class A and Class B funds. If you do decide to buy a Class C fund, take an even more careful look at all loads, fees, and expenses, and compare them very closely to those of the Class A and Class B funds.

When you start looking around at load funds, you'll also see Class D, Class E, and Class F shares or maybe some other types of classes. Whenever you see a fund with "Class" in its name, you can be sure you'll be paying loads, as well as additional fees and expenses. Read the fine print of the mutual fund's prospectus, and ask a lot of questions to be sure you understand the commissions, fees, and expenses you will be paying.

Figuring Out Fees

Whether a mutual fund is a load or no-load fund, you will be charged fees for the annual operating costs of a fund. Every fund must pay a professional manager and his research team. All funds also have administrative expenses to manage investors' accounts. Another big part of the fees a mutual fund pays are the costs of trading stocks, bonds, and other assets held by the fund. So let's review the key fees you have to pay to own a mutual fund.

Management Fees

Professional managers must be paid, and the management fees paid to a fund's investment advisors cover their professional fees for portfolio management. Sometimes also other management fees are payable to the advisor's affiliates. Administrative fees directly related to portfolio management also fit under this category.

Distribution [and/or Service] Fees (12b-1)

Fees in this expense category, which are identified in most prospectuses as "12b-1 fees," are paid out of fund assets to cover distribution or marketing expenses. These 12b-1 fees get their name from the SEC rule that authorizes their payment.

The SEC rule allows funds to charge these fees for marketing and selling fund shares, which can include compensating brokers and others who sell fund shares. These fees also pay the costs of advertising, the printing and mailing of prospectuses to new investors, and the printing and mailing of sales literature. In order for a fund to charge these fees, it must be authorized in the fund's documents.

The NASD limits these fees to no more than 0.75 percent of the fund's assets. The most common fee percentage you'll see for 12b-1 fees is 0.25 percent. Most no-load mutual funds do not charge this fee, but you may see this fee if you purchase the mutual fund through a mutual fund supermarket or other third party rather than from the no-load fund directly.

In some prospectuses, you will see that 12b-1 fees
are authorized to include "shareholder service fees."
These fees cover the costs of responding to investor inquiries. These fees can be included as part of a
fund's 12b-1 fees or as part of "Other Expenses."

Other Expenses

You will find any expenses not included under
"Management Fees" or "Distribution or Service
(12b-1) Fees" in the category "Other Expenses." In
addition to shareholder service expenses that are not
already included in the 12b-1 fees, you will find custodial expenses, legal and accounting expenses, transfer agent expenses, and other administrative expenses.

Total Annual Fund Operating Expenses ("Expense Ratio")

At the bottom of the fee table in the prospectus
you will see the line "Total Annual Fund Operating
Expenses" or "Expense Ratio." This figure represents
the total of a fund's entire annual fund operating
expenses. Each year this Expense Ratio is calculated
based on the total net assets held by the mutual fund.
Use this expense ratio to compare a fund's annual
expenses to other mutual funds you are considering.

Now, let's show you how to use this expense ratio to
calculate long-term costs for your mutual fund portfolio.

Fund Facts

You may find some funds that call themselves "no-load" but really aren't. While it's true the fund does not charge a load (sales commission), it may not be true that you won't pay costs for marketing the fund.

If you see a 12b-1 fee listed in the fund's prospectus, that means you are paying the costs of marketing the fund each year. According to NASD rules, no-load funds can't charge more than 0.25 percent in 12b-1 fees and still be considered a no-load. No-load funds can also charge purchase fees, redemption fees, exchange fees, and account fees, none of which is considered to be a "sales load."

How Commissions and Fees Impact Your Returns

You may think that a 1 or 2 percent fee for managing your portfolio doesn't seem too bad. Well, think again. Commissions and fees can be a drag on your portfolio's long-term earning potential, and the lower you can keep the commissions and fees, the better it is for you.

In fact, a load mutual fund for which you paid a 5.75 percent front-end load (one of the most common loads) with 2 percent annual operating expenses can cost you more than $27,000 in lost earnings over 20 years on an investment of $10,000 versus a no-load index fund with annual fees of only 0.18 percent (the annual fees for Vanguard's popular Index 500 fund).

You may hold a mutual fund for 20 years, or even more, if you're saving for retirement. Why even consider taking such an unnecessary loss when there are more than enough solid no-load mutual funds from which to choose?

To help you understand how dramatically fees can impact the returns on your investment, we've developed four charts that you can find in Figures 4-1, 4-2, 4-3, and 4-4 using the SEC's mutual fund fee calculator (www.sec.gov/investor/tools/mfcc/mfcc-int.htm). Two of these tables compare the costs of a no-load and a load fund held for 10 years, and the other two tables compare a load and no-load fund held for 20 years. The impact of these fees compounds upon itself the longer you hold the fund.

 Mutual Aids

Before you buy a mutual fund, compare the costs of your mutual fund options using the SEC's mutual fund fee calculator (www.sec.gov/investor/tools/mfcc/mfcc-int.htm). Be certain you know what you will be paying in fees throughout the time you will hold that fund. Don't only be concerned about the fees you'll pay when you purchase the fund.

Figure 4-1

Impact of Mutual Fund Fees on a $10,000 Investment
Held in Fund for 10 Years at Average 11% Per Year Return Rate
No Load Mutual Fund

Fee Percentage	Total Fees	Foregone Earnings	Value after 10 Years
0.18%	$349.10	$185.80	$27,859.31
0.5%	$903.62	$484.57	$27,006.02
1%	$1,759.75	$955.25	$25,679.21
1.5%	$2,570.43	$1,412.42	$24,411.37
2%	$3,337.62	$1,856.45	$23,200.14

This table looks at the impact of fees on a no-load mutual fund investment of $10,000 over a 10-year period. We used an average 11 percent annual rate of return, which is the average rate of return that you can expect with a stock fund invested for the long term. We developed the table using the SEC's mutual fund fee calculator.

Figure 4-2

Impact of Mutual Fund Fees on a $10,000 Investment Held in Fund for 10 Years at Average 11% Per Year Return Rate Mutual Fund with 5.75% Front Sales Load			
Fee Percentage	Total Fees	Foregone Earnings	Value after 10 Years
0.18%	$886.88	$1,223.61	$26,283.72
0.5%	$1,426.66	$1,514.37	$25,453.17
1%	$2,223.56	$1,957.99	$24,202.66
1.5%	$2,997.63	$2,388.87	$23,007.71
2%	$3,720.71	$2,807.37	$21,866.13

This table looks at the impact of commissions and fees on a load mutual fund investment of $10,000 over a 10-year period. We used an average 11 percent annual rate of return, which is the average rate of return that you can expect with a stock fund invested for the long term. We developed the table using the SEC's mutual fund fee calculator.

Figure 4-3

| Impact of Mutual Fund Fees on a $10,000 Investment Held in Fund for 20 Years at Average 11% Per Year Return Rate |||
| No Load Mutual Fund ||||
Fee Percentage	Total Fees	Foregone Earnings	Value after 10 Years
0.18%	$1,253.72	$1,599.61	$77,769.78
0.5%	$3,343.95	$4,346.65	$72,932.52
1%	$6,278.65	$8,402.26	$65,942.21
1.5%	$8,845.19	$12,186.45	$59,591.48
2%	$11,080.94	$15,717.54	$53,824.63

This table looks at the impact of fees on a no-load mutual fund investment of $10,000 over a 20-year period. We used an average 11 percent annual rate of return, which is the average rate of return that you can expect with a stock fund invested for the long term. We developed the table using the SEC's mutual fund fee calculator.

Figure 4-4

	Impact of Mutual Fund Fees on a $10,000 Investment Held in Fund for 20 Years at Average 11% Per Year Return Rate Mutual Fund with 5.75% Front Sales Load		
Fee Percentage	Total Fees	Foregone Earnings	Value after 10 Years
0.18%	$1,756.63	$5,568.47	$73,298.02
0.5%	$3,726.67	$8,157.55	$68,738.90
1%	$6,492.63	$11,979.96	$62,150.53
1.5%	$8,911.59	$15,546.56	$56,164.97
2%	$11,018.79	$18,874.61	$50,729.72

This table looks at the impact of commissions and fees on a load mutual fund investment of $10,000 over a 20-year period. We used an average 11 percent annual rate of return, which is the average rate of return that you can expect with a stock fund invested for the long term. We developed the table using the SEC's mutual fund fee calculator.

When you look at these figures, note that the fee percentage starts with 0.18 percent, which is the annual operating expenses for Vanguard's 500 Index Fund. This was the first index fund on the market, and it continues to operate at one of the lowest expense ratios in the mutual fund world. We also used annual fee percentages of 0.5 percent, 1 percent, 1.5 percent, and 2 percent, which represent the most common range of fees. For the load funds, we used 5.75 percent front-end load, which is the most common commission or sales load rate for load mutual funds.

You will find fees differ much more than those shown here. These tables give you at least some ballpark numbers to work with. You should actually use the calculator with your exact commissions, fees, and expected rate of return to figure out how fees and commissions will impact your fund's earnings.

In breaking down the commissions and fees, we have a column called "Costs." This represents the actual fees and commissions you'll pay. Next to that we have a column called "Foregone Earnings." This represents the earnings you lost because of the money paid in fees and expenses.

For example, if you pay a 5.75 percent front load on $10,000, then $575 is taken out before the money is used to buy mutual fund shares. With a front load, you start out with only $9,425 in your account, while someone who chose a no-load mutual fund starts out with the full $10,000. An investor who chooses a load fund is already $575 behind the no-load mutual fund investor. The earnings you would have made on that $575 are "foregone." You'll never be able to make money on them.

Now, let's compare two funds that you plan to hold for 10 years using these tables. In both cases you plan to invest $10,000. Suppose both funds charge an annual rate of 1 percent. One of the funds is a no-load, and the other fund has a front load of 5.75 percent. How much money will you have in 10 years?

First let's look at the results for a no-load fund. Looking at Figure 4-1, you can see that you would have a total of $25,679.21 in 10 years. You would have paid a total of $1,759.75 in fees and would have lost $955.25 in earnings that could not be made on those lost fees.

Now let's look at the results for a load fund. Looking at Figure 4-2, you can see that you would have a total of $24,202.66. You would have paid $2,223.56 in commissions and fees, and you would have lost $1,957.99 in foregone earnings. The only way to surpass the results of the no-load fund would be for you to find a fund with lower fees or one with a higher average total return.

You can look at how fees and commissions impact this same investment in Figures 4-3 and 4-4. Looking at the results for the no-load mutual fund in 20 years in Figure 4-3, you can see the total value of your fund will be $65,942.21, while the load fund shown in Figure 4-4 is worth only $62,150.53—$3,791.68 less. The only difference between what was invested in these two funds and paid out in fees and commissions is the $575 paid in commissions up front. Wow, now that shows you the power of compounding returns!

The difference is much greater if you compare investing $10,000 in a low-cost, no-load index mutual fund with a total annual fee of just 0.18 percent versus a front-end load mutual fund with a load of 5.75 percent plus an annual expense ratio of 2 percent. The low-cost no-load would be worth $77,769.78 at the end of 20 years, while the load fund would be worth only $50,729.72—a difference of $27,040.06.

 Mutual Aids

> Always remember to check out the impact of fees and commissions before you buy any mutual fund. If you are considering two funds that both meet your investment goals, both have managers that have been around for five years or more, and both have similar performance histories—choose the fund with the lower fees.

We just want to show you one other example of how to use the mutual fund cost calculator. In this example, we compare two versions of the same fund—Fidelity's technology sector fund. One of Fidelity's technology sector funds, Fidelity Select Technology, is a no-load with an annual expense ratio of 0.99 percent. Fidelity also offers a load fund with a 5.75 percent front-end load, called Fidelity

Advisor Technology, with an annual expense of 1.37 percent. The primary difference in the expense ratios is a 0.25 12b-1 fee charged for the Fidelity Advisor Technology fund.

The Select fund's five-year average return was 7.05, while the Advisor's five-year average annual return was 8.08. The funds do have different portfolio managers. Looking at these returns, you might think it was worth paying the load for the better returns. Nope!

We put these numbers into the SEC's mutual fund cost calculator and found that even though the no-load fund had a lower average rate of return over the five-year period, investors who chose the no-load fund Fidelity Select Technology had more money in the fund at the end of the five years. Select investors had a total of $13,376.07 while Fidelity Advisor Technology investors only had $12,973.38 in the fund. The higher fees and front-end load reduced the earnings below the no-load investors even though the average five-year rate of return was higher. We had to use the shorter time frame for this example because the Advisor fund only has a five-year history.

To do a similar study comparing two funds, you need to collect this basic information from the mutual fund prospectuses:

1. Total Annual Operating Expenses or Expense Ratio

2. Average annual rate of return. It's best to compare at least a 10-year return rate if you

have it for both funds. If you don't have
a 10-year return rate, pick an equivalent
period of returns. Don't use a 10-year average annual return rate for one fund and a
5-year average annual return rate for another
fund, because returns can differ so greatly
during two different time periods.

3. Front- or back-end load rate, if any.

4. The number of years you plan to invest.

5. The amount you plan to invest.

6. The type of fund—stock, bond, or money
   market.

Now that you understand the impact of commissions and fees on your mutual fund investments,
let's get started with how to research those 8,000
funds and narrow down your options.

The Least You Need to Know

- You must pay operating expenses for all
  mutual funds, but these expenses can vary
  greatly from fund to fund.

- Sales commissions or loads reduce the
  amount of money you invest in mutual funds
  and can be a long-term drag on your funds'
  earnings.

- Pay close attention to mutual fund commissions (loads) and fees. Keep them as low as
  possible so your funds can earn more money
  for you.

How to Research Mutual Funds

In This Chapter

- Research tools and techniques
- Checking out managers
- The use of Internet tools
- Key information options
- Library research

Researching mutual funds is a massive task. There are more than 8,000 mutual funds on the market, and depending on how you count them, you can actually find more than 9,000. However, many of these additional funds are different versions of the same fund with a slight twist.

How can you possibly sort through all these choices and find the right ones for you? Don't get discouraged by the numbers. Luckily, we have some great tools to make this task manageable. But do expect to do some serious work picking funds.

The good news is that you don't have to monitor your fund picks daily or weekly as you would need to do when managing a stock portfolio. You can do a good job of managing your mutual fund portfolio by reviewing it a couple times a year. We talk more about portfolio management in Chapter 8.

In this chapter, we focus on the tools for researching mutual funds and how to use them. In Chapters 6 and 7, we show you how to hone these tools to match your individual investing strategies.

Researching Your Fund Picks

Research, research, and more research is how you manage your own mutual fund portfolio. You first need to do your homework, establish your goals, and come up with a long-term investing plan. We actually tell you how to develop your personal strategies in the next chapter.

But first you need the tools to implement those strategies as you develop them. The tools we discuss in this chapter will give you the skills you need to research the mutual fund choices that you think will best meet your investing goals.

You won't use these tools just once, but over and over again as you monitor your mutual fund portfolio through the years. You always want to know the funds you have chosen are performing well and that their managers and management strategies continue to handle the fund as you expect, based on the goals and strategies you chose.

Finding the Right Manager

Ultimately, what you want to do is find the right professional portfolio managers to manage your money. These are the people who will actually decide what stocks, bonds, and other assets to put in the mutual fund portfolios whose shares you buy.

The fees you pay for management, which should be your primary costs for owning funds (see Chapter 4 for more details on mutual fund costs), will go primarily to the professional portfolio managers who manage each of the funds you choose.

As you start your research, look at several key things:

- **Fund Type**   Sort out your possible choices by looking at fund type, such as domestic or international stock fund; government, corporate, or municipal bond fund; growth fund; value fund; or balanced fund. There are many more types of mutual funds, which we cover in detail in Chapter 2.

- **Performance**   Review a fund's performance over the past year, as well as over the past 5 years and past 10 years, if available. You'll likely be holding these funds for the long haul, so you want to know how the fund has done for longer than just the past year. While past performance is no guarantee of future performance, it's a good indicator of how well the mutual fund manager has managed his portfolio. As you dig deeper into the fund, look at the tenure of the manager.

The fund may have changed managers, and the past performance may no longer be relevant. The new manager will likely change the portfolio to his liking.

● **Costs**   Review the total cost for investing in each of your possible fund choices. We talk more about how to test those costs and determine their long-term impact on your portfolio in Chapter 4.

● **Ratings and Risks**   Review the mutual funds' ratings and risks. We talk more about ratings later when we discuss how to use the best screener for finding funds—Morningstar's Fund Screener.

● **Asset Turnover and Market Cap**   When you research stock mutual funds, consider how frequently assets are turned over (which means how often they are bought and sold). If a fund manager trades his assets frequently, that can add dramatically to the costs of operating the fund because it increases the operating expenses for the fund, which ultimately will reduce your portfolio's potential for growth. In addition to asset turnover, consider market cap, which relates to how large the companies are that your mutual fund manager picks for his portfolio. A portfolio of primarily small companies will have very different performance results than a portfolio of primarily large corporations. Small companies tend to be more volatile than large companies, but they also have a greater potential for long-term growth. It's good to have a mix of market cap sizes in your mutual fund portfolio. As you research the funds, find the best funds for each market cap size.

● **Credit Quality and Duration**   When you research potential bond funds, search by credit quality and duration (or maturity) of the assets the portfolio manager chooses for the bond fund's portfolio. Bond funds built using higher-credit-quality bonds are safer but will have lower rates of return than those funds with lower-quality bonds. We talk more about the different types of bond funds in Chapter 2.

Using these various screening criteria, you can narrow your fund choices from 8,000 to probably 5 to 10 good choices for your portfolio within each mutual fund type you want to buy. Once you've narrowed down your list, get copies of the mutual fund prospectuses for each of the potential candidates, and start researching each one more deeply.

Also find out what analysts say about the fund's past performance, as well as where they believe the fund is going. In these analytical reports, you'll find discussion about the manager and how well he manages his fund. You'll also find out how long he has managed the fund. In addition, you want to monitor any management changes that could impact the future performance of the fund.

Using the Internet

By far the best source for researching mutual funds on the Internet is Morningstar, which is the leading independent investment research firm for mutual fund shareholders. Morningstar also serves financial advisors and institutional clients, such as pension fund managers.

On its website at www.morningstar.com, you'll find information about stocks, variable annuities, *closed-end mutual funds*, *exchange-traded funds*, *hedge funds*, and *529 college savings plans*.

Categorizing Funds

Morningstar is famous for its "star" ratings, which rate funds within their established categories based on the way the fund actually invests its money. While you may read in a fund's prospectus that its investment strategies involve buying the stock of large companies with growth potential, you may find that Morningstar categorizes the fund differently after looking at the actual stocks owned by the fund.

You can get an overview of the Morningstar fund categories and their performance at http://news. morningstar.com/fundReturns/CategoryReturns. html?fsection=ListCatPerformance. If you have difficulty using this link, you can find the fund category performance chart by clicking on the "Funds" tab from the main page of www.morningstar.com. You'll then see the link for category returns under "Mutual Fund Performance" in the right column.

def•i•ni•tion

Closed-end mutual funds are funds in which a fixed number of shares are sold at an initial public offering (IPO). After that IPO, these funds are traded more like stocks than are open-end mutual funds.

Exchange-traded funds (ETFs) are funds that track a specific stock exchange index, such as the S&P 500 index. ETFs bundle together the securities in that index and trade the package in the same way that stock is bought and sold.

Hedge funds are usually used solely by wealthy individuals and institutions that want to find a money manager who will use aggressive and riskier investing strategies. Most hedge funds are exempt from many of the rules governing mutual funds. Investors usually need at least $100,000 to get into a hedge fund.

529 College Savings Plans were designed to give parents a way to save for their children's education without taxation on growth of the funds. The funds withdrawn from these plans also are tax-free, provided the funds are used for qualified education programs.

Once you are on the category page, pick a category that interests you. When you click on the category name, you will find a list of the best funds in that category. The chart gives the 1-month, year-to-date, 3-month, 1-year, 3-year, and 5-year rates of return for each of the funds on the list. You can compare those returns to the same average returns for the category, so you know how each fund is doing in relation to its category.

If you want to dig even deeper, click on a fund name and get a snapshot of the fund. As part of this snapshot, you'll find additional links to much more free information, including information about Morningstar's Rating, Total Returns, Tax Analysis, Risk Measures, Portfolio, Management, Fees & Expenses, and Purchase Information.

You do have to pay for some information, such as analyst research and stewardship grade. The stewardship grade includes reviews of the fund family and how they operate. This is part of premium membership with Morningstar, which is well worth the cost if you plan to invest using mutual funds.

 Mutual Aids

While a lot of good information is free on Morningstar's website, you will have to pay for some information through its premium membership. You can try out the premium membership for two weeks for free. After the trial period, you can get monthly membership for $14.95 per month and yearly membership for $135.

In addition to excellent analyst research, you get excellent portfolio management tools with Morningstar's premium membership. We talk about those tools and how to use them in Chapter 8.

Screening Funds

While looking for funds in categories is certainly one method for locating possible fund choices, an easier and less tedious method is using a mutual fund screening tool. We introduced you to categories first, so you'll understand how to set up the screening tool.

To use a mutual fund screening tool, first set up the criteria for your search. Then you can see the results, score them, and revise the scoring priorities to meet your criteria.

You can set a number of criteria. In each criterion, you have the option to leave it at the default "any" so you don't have to make a choice in each of these criteria areas. Here's an overview of the criteria choices you'll find when you start working with Morningstar's Mutual Fund Screener:

- **Fund Type** When you use these criteria, you can pick the fund group, whether domestic stock, international stock, taxable bond, municipal bond, or balanced. You can also leave it on the default option "all," but we don't recommend it because you'll end up with too many choices and negate the value of the tool. After picking the fund type, you'll be shown the list of Morningstar Categories that fit the fund type. You can select a category or leave it on "all." The third choice is manager tenure, with categories of average, 1-year, 3-year, 5-year, or 10-year. Whatever time span you pick, the choices will match that time span or longer.

- **Cost and Purchase** You can select a minimum initial purchase ranging from $500 to $10,000. If you have only $500 to invest right now, select that one. It will limit the options to funds that accept that minimum purchase, but others won't be worth looking at right now anyway. Next, make a choice between load funds or no-load funds. We certainly recommend you focus your search on no-load funds. Finally, select your expense ratio, which will be less than or equal to the amount you select. A good place to start is 1 percent; that way you will knock out any funds with annual operating costs over that percentage. You should only consider going above that cost percentage if you can't find acceptable funds that operate more cheaply. We talk more about the impact of these costs in Chapter 4.

- **Ratings and Risk** Here you can pick the Morningstar Star Ratings you will consider. Morningstar's top ratings in each category are four and five stars, which is a good place to start. If you don't find anything acceptable, you can always take a look at the three-star funds by doing another search. If you're looking in an area where you think there may be a lot of new funds you want to consider, then also select the "New, unrated funds" category. You also can make a selection regarding risk. Options for risks include low, below average, average, above average, and high. This is a personal preference based on how much risk you want to take. The higher the risk the greater the rewards in most cases, but you also risk a greater possibility of experiencing a loss in your portfolio value if the market turns against your choices.

- **Returns** You can set return expectations for year-to-date, 1-year, 3-year, 5-year, and 10-year. Category options in each of these criteria include average, S&P 500, or you can type in a rate of return you seek.

- **Stock funds** You can set a turnover ratio (which measures how frequently the portfolio is traded) and a total assets size (where you can indicate whether you prefer a certain size mutual fund). Some people do believe larger funds offer less growth, while others prefer large funds because their operating costs are usually lower.

- **Bond funds** You can make choices based on credit quality of the bonds and on the duration for which the bonds are held.

Yes, this does seem like a lot of choices, especially when you're first learning how to use mutual funds. But you don't have to make a choice for each criterion. You can focus on three or four and still narrow your options considerably.

For example, always pick the fund group, but skip the category and manager tenure if that's not a critical factor for your initial screening. If you do have a minimum initial purchase level that is critical to your choice, pick that or otherwise just leave it on "any." We do suggest you search for no-load mutual funds and pick an expense ratio of less than or equal to one.

Ratings and Risk are personal choices. If you want the best funds in the category you're selecting, then choose four- and five-star funds, but three-star funds can also offer some good options. We recommend you stay away from one- and two-star funds. Those ratings usually indicate a significant problem within the fund.

When it comes to returns, we suggest you pick one that matches your goal. For example, if you plan to hold the fund for at least 10 years, you may want to select an option ranking them by better than the category average for 10 years. That way the funds at the top of the list will be those doing better than the average for the category you're considering.

Leave portfolio specifics for bond and stock funds at the default "any" mode until you better understand the mutual fund world and your personal preferences. Your goal is to get this initial screen down to a manageable number of funds for you to research and make choices for purchase.

Running the Mutual Fund Screen Tool

Use these four steps to find your top 10 mutual fund choices for a particular fund type:

- **Step 1**   When you've made all your criteria choices, then click on the "Show Results" tab to see how you did. Hopefully you've narrowed your choices to about 25 to 30 funds.

- **Step 2**   When you get the results, the next step is to score the results. Click on the tab that says "Score Results." Then you'll get a screen that will allow you to prioritize some of the criteria on a 10-point scale. For example, since low cost is critical, you want to score that one at 10. When you change it from the medium level of 5, you will see your choices jump around to move up the funds that have the lowest costs. You then might want to change the priority on a high 5-year return, so you can move that one from an importance of 5 to 10.

- **Step 3**   Now you have a list of the top 10 funds that meet your criteria for the search. Next, click on the tab that says "Fund Detail Results" to get a summary of the funds you've picked. You can look at those results using several different views. A good choice of view is one called "Performance View." That one will show your top ranked funds along with their performance year-to-date, as well as 1-month, 3-month, 1-year, 3-year, and 5-year.

- **Step 4**   You can click on the link to the specific funds that interest you on the list and go to the snapshot page for the fund. From that page you will be able to find a lot more free information about Morningstar's Rating,

Total Returns, Tax Analysis, Risk Measures, Portfolio, Management, Fees & Expenses, and Purchase Information.

Using this fund-screening tool, you can quickly narrow your choices to a reasonable number that you can then research more deeply to find just the right one to meet your investment goals. You should at least try the free premium subscription for two weeks to see whether or not the additional information, especially the analyst research, will be valuable for you. You can find reports dating back 10 years or more if Morningstar has covered the fund that long.

When you have premium access, you also have access to Morningstar's Picks and Pans on the mutual funds page, which can be a good way to narrow your choices. Morningstar premium users also have access to an excellent cost analyzer that can compare the costs of five funds directly related to criteria you based on your personal investing situation.

Checking Out More Key Information Sources

In addition to Morningstar, you may want to check out a number of excellent sources for additional information.

Kiplinger's Personal Finance (www.kiplinger. com/personalfinance/investing/funds)

You can find excellent coverage of the mutual fund industry and mutual fund investing at Kiplinger's Personal Finance. The website provided here takes you directly to the mutual fund page, but do explore the site for other personal finance stories as well. You will find good information about investing for retirement and investing for your child's education. You can access Kiplinger's stories for free.

Barron's (online.barrons.com/public/main)

Barron's is published by the *Wall Street Journal* and focuses specifically on investor issues. You will find excellent information at Barron's, but you do have to pay for it. You can try it out for 30 days for free. After that you can get an annual subscription to the Internet content for $79.

The No-Load Fund Investor (www. sheldonjacobs.com)

The No-Load Fund Investor is a comprehensive newsletter that tracks 996 no-load funds and ETFs. In this newsletter you'll find data, comparative reports of performance, and specific recommendations. You also can follow the performance of model portfolios targeted to different investing goals and lifestyle choices. An annual subscription to the newsletter is regularly $199, but you can try it out for the first time at a reduced rate of $129.

You can also find some good newsletters that focus on specific fund families. For example, Vanguard mutual fund shareholders may find the *Independent*

Advisor for Vanguard Investors (www.adviseronline. com) useful. A good newsletter for Fidelity mutual fund shareholders is *Fidelity Investor* (www. fidelityinvestor.com).

Using the libraries

While we have focused extensively on using the Internet in this chapter, you probably can research mutual funds at your local library. What you'll find at your local library will depend on the research sources the library decides to carry.

Check with your local librarian to find out what is available in your library. He also may be able to recommend another branch or possibly a local community college or university that may have more resources.

In addition to the publications mentioned in this chapter, another good source you may find at the library is Value Line. We didn't recommend their website because very little of it can be accessed online for free. Most of Value Line's information must be purchased either for electronic use (a computer disc) or in paper form. Annual subscription fees exceed $300. But there is a good chance that your library does carry Value Line publications that you will be able to access there for free.

The Least You Need to Know

- Taking the time to properly research funds is critical to your success in choosing mutual funds that will meet your goals and needs.

- On the Internet, the best tool you can use for narrowing down funds that meet your criteria is Morningstar's Mutual Fund Finder. Take the time to learn how to use it.

- Other sources for researching funds include your public library, Barron's, Kiplinger's, and various mutual fund newsletters.

Chapter

Investing Strategically: Understanding Asset Allocation

In This Chapter
- Exploring asset allocation
- Buy and hold versus market timing
- Producing results
- Tool when picking funds

Now that you are familiar with all the key pieces of the mutual fund pie—types, buying, costs, and research techniques—let's put all this together to invest wisely, based on your goals for your portfolio.

In this chapter, I discuss the key investment strategy you should use—*asset allocation*, which can help you build a strong portfolio for the long term. I also discuss buy and hold investing versus market timing.

What Does Asset Allocation Mean?

You may think that picking top-performing mutual funds is the answer for building the best long-term portfolio, but that is not the case. Many academic studies have shown that the actual mutual funds chosen account for just 5 to 10 percent of your portfolio's success, while 90 to 95 percent can be attributed to the allocation of your portfolio among the types of funds you pick, including stock, bond, money market, and balanced mutual funds.

def•i•ni•tion

Asset allocation is the process of dividing up your assets among different types of investments, including stocks, bonds, real estate, and cash, in order to minimize your risks and optimize your returns.

You should consider five key things as you determine the right asset allocation for you—your investment goal, your investment horizon, your risk tolerance, your financial resources, and your investment mix. Let's take a closer look at these five factors.

Your Investment Goal

First and foremost, determine the reason you are investing. You may want to save for retirement, for education, for the down payment on your first home, or for any other purpose that meets your needs.

You must decide on your goals and when you will need the money before you can even begin to plan the rest of your investment strategy.

Your Investment Horizon

Your investment time horizon involves the number of years you have before you need the money. Once you have determined your goal(s), the time horizon is easy to calculate.

For example, if you want to save for retirement and know you have 20 to 30 years before you will retire, you can develop an aggressive asset allocation for your portfolio because you can ride out the highs and lows of a volatile stock market. You won't be forced to sell assets to get cash in a down market because you can wait for the market to recover before selling assets.

But if your primary goal is to save for a home and you'll need the money in five years, you don't want to take much risk of facing a dip in the stock market just as you are ready to withdraw the money from your mutual funds for your home purchase. In that case, you are better off with a bond or money market mutual fund.

Saving for educational expenses usually falls somewhere in between these retirement and home-buying goals. In this case, the amount of time you have before you need the money will depend on when your child will need the money.

When you are investing, time can either be your best friend or your biggest enemy. If you have 10 or more years before you need the money, you can take a lot of risk because you can wait until the market recovers from a downturn. If you need the money in two years, you don't want to take any unnecessary risk because you don't have time to wait for a market turnaround.

If you need the money soon, your primary concern should be preservation of principal. The last thing you want to face is being forced to sell an asset at a loss just because you need the money. Don't get me wrong, there will be times when you have to accept your losses and move on if you made a bad investment choice; but you don't want to be forced to do this just because you don't have the time to wait for better market conditions.

Mutual Aids

As you get closer to the time you will need your money, you should move your money into less volatile investments. You don't want to get stuck in the stock or bond markets and be forced to sell your holdings when stocks or bonds are down. By allocating your funds carefully, you won't have to worry about taking a significant loss just because you were in a rush to get your funds.

Generally, we recommend that if you need the money in two years, you should save the money in a cash equivalent, such as a money market mutual fund, so you know that your principal is safe and you don't have to worry about a dip in the market.

If your time horizon is two to five years down the road, you can consider using a bond mutual fund or a balanced mutual fund. While you do take some risk that the market will take a dip during that period, you will have enough time to wait out a downward turn. As you get nearer to needing the money in less than two years, you should sell the bond or balanced mutual fund shares and buy shares in a money market mutual fund.

If you have five or more years until you'll need the money, then you can invest more aggressively in stock mutual funds. You should start to look for the best opportunity to sell those stock mutual funds and buy less volatile bond or balanced funds once you are within five years of needing the money. Then finally switch to money market funds as you get within two years of withdrawing the cash.

Your Risk Tolerance

Ask yourself, "How much risk can I take and still be able to sleep at night?" To help you figure out your answer to this question and determine your risk tolerance, ask yourself these questions:

- Do market fluctuations keep you awake at night?
- Are you unfamiliar with investing?

- Do you consider yourself more a saver than an investor?
- Are you fearful of losing 25 percent of your assets in a few days or weeks?

If you answered "yes" to these questions, you likely are a "conservative" investor.

- Are you comfortable with the ups and downs of the securities markets?
- Are you knowledgeable about investing and the securities markets?
- Are you investing for long-term goals?
- Can you withstand considerable short-term losses?

If you answered "yes" to these questions, you are likely to be an "aggressive" investor. Or if you fall somewhere in between the two, you can call yourself a "moderate" investor.

As we discuss how to use asset allocation to produce better results, remember that if you are a conservative investor, don't pick the most aggressive portfolio mix—even if you like the results. If you have a low risk tolerance and pick mutual funds that are too aggressive, you likely will want to sell them at the first market downturn rather than lose a lot of money. If you can tolerate greater risks, your results will be better with a more aggressive mix of primarily stock mutual funds.

Your Financial Resources

The amount you have to invest will also be a factor in the risk you might want to take. In order to invest directly in stocks and bonds using good asset allocation strategies, you need to have a lot of money. Luckily, mutual funds can give you a good asset allocation mix even if you only have a few hundred dollars to invest.

Portfolio Mix

The portfolio mix involves the percentage that you hold in each of the mutual fund types you select. For example, if you hold 100 percent of your portfolio in stock mutual funds, that can be a risky portfolio with a good chance for growth but also a greater possibility of loss if the stock market drops in value.

If you hold 100 percent of your portfolio in money market funds, you don't have to worry about losing any principal, but you won't get a very good return on your investment. When using good asset allocation strategies, you develop your investment strategies by deciding how much risk you can take and then mixing your mutual fund holdings among stock mutual funds, bond mutual funds, and money market mutual funds.

For example, an aggressive investor may decide that he wants to hold 80 percent of his portfolio in stock mutual funds and 20 percent in bond or money market mutual funds. A conservative investor may do exactly the opposite and invest 80 percent of his portfolio in bond or money market mutual funds and only 20 percent in stock mutual funds.

Market Timing vs. Buy and Hold Investing

Another common battle among investors is whether to try to time the market or just buy and hold on to your investments for a long time. While some investors do believe they can improve their odds by trying to time the market, we don't recommend that you try it.

Those who have been most successful in investing believe the buy and hold strategy works the best. In fact, billionaire investor Warren Buffett goes one step further. He recommends that one should buy good companies and hold them "forever."

You probably are not as perfect at picking stocks as Warren Buffett, so the idea of holding a company or a mutual fund forever may not work for you. Knowing when to sell your mutual funds requires regular monitoring of the quarterly reports you receive either from an individual company or from a mutual fund company, depending on the type of investment you select. In the next chapter, we explore how to construct your portfolio; and in Chapter 8, we talk about managing that portfolio.

Fund Facts

One of the world's most respected investors is billionaire Warren Buffett, who is chairman and CEO of Berkshire Hathaway. He says in the Owner's Manual for his stockholders, "As owners of, say, Coca-Cola or Gillette shares, we think of Berkshire as being a nonmanaging partner in two extraordinary businesses, in which we measure our success by the long-term progress of the companies rather than by the month-to-month movements of their stocks. In fact, we would not care in the least if several years went by in which there was no trading, or quotation of prices, in the stocks of those companies. If we have good long-term expectations, short-term price changes are meaningless for us except to the extent they offer us an opportunity to increase our ownership at an attractive price."

How Does Asset Allocation Help Produce Results?

What is the best asset allocation? That all depends on the number of years you have before you need the money. Stocks historically have averaged 11.3 percent; bonds have averaged 5.1 percent; and cash deposits have averaged 3 percent.

Now let's take a look at how to use these historical averages to figure out the likely results for a sample portfolio. A moderate portfolio balanced for growth would likely have 60 percent stock, 20 percent bonds, and 20 percent cash. Using these returns as the average, the portfolio would likely earn 8.4 percent before taxes and inflation. This is what we call a weighted average.

Here is how you calculate that weighted average:

> 60 percent stock funds at 11.3 percent
>
> > $11.3 \times .60$ = 6.78 percent
>
> 20 percent bond funds at 5.1 percent
>
> > $5.1 \times .20$ = 1.02 percent
>
> 20 percent cash at 3 percent
>
> > $3.0 \times .20$ <u>= .60 percent</u>
> >
> > Total = 8.40 percent

Suppose you are saving for retirement and are in your 20s or 30s; you have a long way to go before needing the funds. At this stage in life you can afford to take more risks because you have more time to recover from a drop in the stock market.

You decide you want an aggressive growth portfolio. You don't want to put all your money in stock mutual funds because that's a higher risk than you can tolerate. Instead you decide to put 80 percent of your portfolio in stock mutual funds and 20 percent in bond mutual funds. What would the likely results of this portfolio be, based on historical returns?

Here's how you calculate the weighted average for that portfolio:

> 80 percent stock funds at 11.3 percent
>
> $$11.3 \times .80 = 9.04 \text{ percent}$$
>
> 20 percent bond funds at 5.1 percent
>
> $$5.1 \times .20 = 1.02 \text{ percent}$$
>
> Total $= 10.06$ percent

You can see that with this more aggressive portfolio, you will have a 1.66 percent higher return each year than you would have had with a more moderate 60/20/20 split shown above.

If you are in your 50s and 60s, you are much closer to retirement and, therefore, want to be more cautious about the risks you take. You might prefer the 60/20/20 split or even a 50/50 split between stock mutual funds and bond mutual funds.

Here's the weighted average for a 50 percent stock mutual funds and 50 bond mutual funds portfolio:

> 50 percent stock funds at 11.3 percent
>
> $$11.3 \times .50 = 5.65 \text{ percent}$$
>
> 50 percent bond funds at 5.1 percent
>
> $$5.1 \times .50 = 2.55 \text{ percent}$$
>
> Total $= 8.2$ percent

It is generally believed that for people in their 20s and 30s, an allocation of 70 to 80 percent in stock or stock funds and 20 to 30 percent in bonds or money market funds is a good mix that will build a solid retirement portfolio for the future. As you get closer to retirement, you should gradually shift that allocation when you're 5 to 10 years away from retirement. That way you can reallocate your assets when the market conditions are right for selling each of the riskier assets you hold.

Remember the old adage, "Buy low; sell high." As you look to reallocate your portfolio, remember to sell assets at one of their highs and not when that type of asset is generally at a low. Give yourself 5 to 10 years to reallocate your portfolio. That way you are not forced to sell an asset in a down phase just because you need the money.

In retirement, most planners believe there should still be some growth stocks in your portfolio because people are living 20 years or more in retirement and you don't want to run out of money. A good allocation in retirement actually reverses the allocation for folks in their 20s and 30s. For retirement it is wise to have 20 to 30 percent in stocks or stock funds and 70 to 80 percent in bonds, bond funds, or money market funds. If you think you'll be living 20 years in retirement, you may even consider a 50/50 split for your portfolio.

How You Use Asset Allocation to Pick Your Funds

In addition to looking at whether you should buy a stock, bond, or money market mutual fund, you also need to mix the type of stock, bond, and money market funds you pick.

For example, as we discussed in Chapter 2, stock mutual funds can have very different investing goals, such as growth, value, sector-specific, or international. So you want to allocate your assets among various types of stock funds as well.

Mix growth, value, and international mutual fund choices, so you can take advantage of the ups and downs of the market. Often when growth stocks are soaring, value stocks have very low returns. When U.S. stocks are down, often you'll find international stocks are up. By allocating your assets among these various types of stock mutual funds, you can minimize the volatility of your portfolio.

Fund Fears

Sector mutual funds are always the most volatile and risky, but if you believe that a particular sector will give you the growth you want, you can always put a small percentage of your portfolio into sector funds. Just don't overload your portfolio with them unless you plan to closely manage the portfolio on a monthly or more frequent basis.

You should also consider your portfolio mix for your bond funds. For example, bond funds that invest primarily in short-term bonds (bonds that mature in one to three years) will go up when funds that invest in long-term bonds go down and vice versa. By mixing up the type of bond funds you select, you can minimize the volatility of your portfolio.

Use these basics about asset allocation and investment mix to pick your mutual funds. As you research possible mutual fund choices, collect information about each fund's 5-year and 10-year average annual returns.

Then as you narrow down your choices, use the weighted average calculation to calculate the returns you can expect, based on your actual choices. This will help you determine your projected returns for your portfolio. We take you through the process of actually constructing your portfolio in the next chapter.

The Least You Need to Know

- Asset allocation is an investment strategy for managing your portfolio.
- Consider five key factors when planning your asset allocation—goals, time horizon, risk tolerance, financial resources, and portfolio mix.
- Use a weighted average calculation to project the returns for your portfolio.

Chapter 7

Constructing Your Mutual Fund Portfolio

In This Chapter

- Goal setting
- Determining types
- Picking funds
- The use of autopilot

Now that you understand the basics of asset allocation, let's work on constructing your portfolio. First, you need to set your goals and then figure out an asset allocation that gives you the best chance of meeting those goals. Finally, you need to select the mutual funds within each of the fund types identified as we walk you through the process of constructing your portfolio.

Setting Your Goals

As you remember in Chapter 6, we discussed the five basic elements of asset allocation:

- Your investment goal
- Your investment horizon
- Your risk tolerance
- Your financial resources
- Your portfolio mix

Now let's look at how these five elements impact the way you construct your portfolio. First and foremost, what is your investment goal? Why do you want to build the portfolio?

Some common goals include:

- Saving to buy a house
- Saving for a child's education
- Saving for retirement
- Saving to start or buy a business

Of course, the list could go on much longer. Think about your goals for how you want to use the money. Also think about when you will need the money. Your time horizon will be critical to determining how much risk you want to take.

As I discussed in Chapter 6, if you need the money in two years or less, you want to invest with minimal risk. You can take on a bit more risk if you need the money in two to five years. You can build a riskier portfolio for money needed in 5 to 10 years, and you can take the greatest amount of risk if you don't need the money for 10 years or more.

Mutual Aids

> While your time horizon means you can take on risks, you may not be able to tolerate the ups and downs of the market, so don't take on more risk than you can psychologically accept. It's more important that you sleep at night and not worry constantly about your investment portfolio. People who take on more risk than they can tolerate usually end up selling at a loss when they panic as the market goes down.

Just because you have the time needed to invest more aggressively and take on more risk, that doesn't mean you must do so. If you are a conservative investor, you won't make the best buy and sell decisions as the market goes down if you construct a riskier portfolio than you can tolerate. You'll become too nervous and end up selling your mutual funds as their values drop rather then ride out the storm and wait for the next recovery.

As you construct your portfolio, the amount you have to start with initially will impact how many different types of mutual funds you can buy. For example, if you're just starting to invest for retirement and can only invest $100 per month, you should start with one good growth mutual fund stock portfolio. As your portfolio increases, you can begin to diversify your holdings.

Generally, you can put together a good asset allocation by holding 5 to 10 mutual funds. You never need to hold more than 10. Remember, good mutual funds are already offering you a well-diversified portfolio.

Picking Fund Types

Once you set your goals, your next step is to decide what types of mutual funds you want in your portfolio. Here are the key types from which you can choose (see Chapter 2 for a full explanation of each):

- Stock Funds—growth, value, sector, and international
- Bond Funds—taxable, tax-free, long-term, short-term, and intermediate-term.
- Money Market Funds
- Balanced or Life Cycle Funds

Now let's look at how to mix up these types into sample portfolios that you can use, based on your goals, horizon, and risk tolerance. I've developed five sample portfolio mixes for you:

Safety

Your portfolio should include:

• Bond Mutual Funds	**60 percent**
Intermediate-term bond funds	30 percent
Long-term bond funds	30 percent

- Stock Funds   **20 percent**
  Growth stock funds   10 percent
  Value stock funds   10 percent
- Cash/Money Market Funds   **20 percent**

If preserving capital is your number-one priority, consider this type of portfolio mix. You likely are someone who needs the money in two years or less or you just can't tolerate the idea that your principal could drop in value.

You can't be guaranteed that your principal won't lose value, but the risk is minimal. The only place you can get an absolute guarantee that you won't lose any of your principal is to deposit your money into an insured bank account, but the return likely will be less.

Two common investment goals for this type of portfolio could be to buy a house in two years or preserve capital and provide an income stream in retirement.

Historical returns for this type of portfolio based on the weighted average calculation, are:

20 percent stock funds at 11.3 percent

$$11.3 \times .20 = 2.26 \text{ percent}$$

60 percent bond funds at 5.1 percent

$$5.1 \times .60 = 3.06 \text{ percent}$$

20 percent cash at 3 percent

$$3.0 \times .20 = \underline{.60 \text{ percent}}$$
$$\text{Total} = 5.92 \text{ percent}$$

Remember, these are historical returns, and nothing guarantees that future returns will match this average. You will see this warning in all mutual fund prospectuses. It's true of any investment in stocks. Bonds do have a guaranteed interest rate, but their value can go up and down as well.

When you are about 12 months from needing the money, start looking for a good time to convert your stock funds to cash. And when you're six months from needing the money, look for a good opportunity to convert your bond funds to cash. This likely will give you the time you need to find an upswing in the stock or bond market so you can sell your holdings without a loss of principal.

Conservative

Your portfolio should include:

- Bond Mutual Funds **45 percent**
  - Intermediate-term bond funds 30 percent
  - Long-term bond funds 15 percent
- Stock Funds **40 percent**
  - Growth stock funds 20 percent
  - Value stock funds 20 percent
- Cash/Money Market Funds **15 percent**

If you won't need the money for two to five years, you can take on a bit more risk and put more of the portfolio in stock funds and less in bond funds. This portfolio will give you a greater chance for growth without taking on much risk.

Historical returns for this type of portfolio based on the weighted average calculation, are:

40 percent stock funds at 11.3 percent

$$11.3 \times .40 = 4.52 \text{ percent}$$

45 percent bond funds at 5.1 percent

$$5.1 \times .45 = 2.3 \text{ percent}$$

15 percent cash at 3 percent

$$3.0 \times .15 = .45 \text{ percent}$$
$$\text{Total} = 7.27 \text{ percent}$$

Once you are about 24 months from needing the money, you should start looking for a good time to convert your stock funds to cash. When you're six months from needing the money, look for a good opportunity to convert your bond funds to cash. This likely will give you the time you need to find an upswing in the stock or bond market so you can sell your holdings without a loss of principal.

Moderate

Your portfolio should include:

- Stock Funds **60 percent**
  - Growth stock funds 30 percent
  - Value stock funds 30 percent
- Bond Mutual Funds **30 percent**
  - Intermediate-term bond funds 15 percent
  - Long-term bond funds 15 percent
- Cash/Money Market Funds **10 percent**

If you have 5 to 10 years before needing the money, you can consider this type of portfolio mix. However, you should have a moderate tolerance for risk because you could face a significant drop in your stock mutual fund holdings if the market takes a downturn.

You need to have the patience to wait out a downturn in the market and not move to sell your holdings at a loss unless you believe you've made a mistake with the funds chosen and want to prevent any further loss. In fact, many investors consider a downturn in the market a good time to buy additional shares of a well-managed mutual fund.

 Fund Fears

If you fear losing your money and can't accept any drop in the value of your principal even for a short period of time, do not consider buying stock mutual funds. As long as you have the time to wait out a storm, you should be able to recover from any loss by holding the fund and waiting for the market to recover.

Historical returns for this type of portfolio based on the weighted average calculation are:

60 percent stock funds at 11.3 percent

$$11.3 \times .60 = 6.78 \text{ percent}$$

30 percent bond funds at 5.1 percent

$$5.1 \times .30 = 1.53 \text{ percent}$$

10 percent cash at 3 percent

$$3.0 \times .10 = \underline{.3 \text{ percent}}$$

Total   = 8.61 percent

When you are about 60 months from needing the money, start looking for a good time to convert some of your stock funds to bonds and shift your asset mix toward the mix shown above in the conservative portfolio. Once you've reallocated to that portfolio, you should then use portfolio strategies for moving to cash, as with the conservative portfolio.

Growth

Your portfolio should include:

- Stock Funds **75 percent**
  Growth stock funds 50 percent
  Value stock funds 15 percent
  International 10 percent
- Bond Mutual Funds **20 percent**
  Large blend bond funds 20 percent
- Cash/Money Market Funds **5 percent**

If you have 10 years or more before you will need the money, such as saving for retirement or your child's education, you can consider a growth portfolio as long as you have a strong tolerance for risk. You will face periods of time when your portfolio does show a loss in principal. You won't actually lose the money as long as you don't sell the funds and instead ride out the storm and wait for the market to rebound.

Historical returns for this type of portfolio based on the weighted average calculation are:

75 percent stock funds at 11.3 percent

$$11.3 \times .75 = 8.48 \text{ percent}$$

20 percent bond funds at 5.1 percent

$$5.1 \times .20 = 1.02 \text{ percent}$$

5 percent cash at 3 percent

$$3.0 \times .05 = \underline{.15 \text{ percent}}$$
$$\text{Total} = 9.65 \text{ percent}$$

When you are about seven years from needing the money, start looking for a good time to convert some of your stock funds to bonds and shift your asset mix toward the mix shown above in the moderate portfolio. Once you've reallocated to that portfolio, you should then use portfolio strategies for managing a moderate portfolio.

Aggressive Growth

Your portfolio should include:

- Stock Funds **90 percent**
  Growth stock funds 50 percent
  Value stock funds 20 percent
  International 20 percent

- Bond Mutual Funds   **5 percent**
    Large blend bond fund   5 percent
- Cash/Money Market Funds   **5 percent**

If you have 10 years or more before you will need the money, such as saving for retirement or your child's education, you can consider an aggressive growth portfolio as long as you have a very strong tolerance for risk. You will face periods of time when your portfolio does show a significant loss in principal, but you won't actually lose the money as long as you don't sell the funds but instead ride out the storm and wait for the market to rebound.

Historical returns for this type of portfolio based on the weighted average calculation are:

90 percent stock funds at 11.3 percent

$$11.3 \times .90 = 10.17 \text{ percent}$$

5 percent bond funds at 5.1 percent

$$5.1 \times .05 = 0.26 \text{ percent}$$

5 percent cash at 3 percent

$$3.0 \times .05 = \underline{0.15 \text{ percent}}$$
$$\text{Total} = 10.58 \text{ percent}$$

When you are about seven years from needing the money, start looking for a good time to convert some of your stock funds to bonds and shift your asset mix toward the mix shown above in the moderate portfolio. Once you've reallocated to that portfolio, use portfolio strategies for managing a moderate portfolio.

Selecting Funds Within Fund Types

After you've picked your portfolio asset mix from one of the model portfolios discussed previously or you decide on your portfolio asset mix, it's time to start picking funds. In Chapter 5, I show you how to pick funds. To practice using these tools, let's pick possible candidates for a Growth portfolio.

We need to pick two stock mutual funds, one that is a growth fund and one that is a value fund. We also need to pick a long-term bond mutual fund. Since there aren't any good no-load international funds that you can get into with just $1,000 to invest, let's move the international fund portion into a value fund.

You really need a minimum of $3,000 to invest in a good no-load international mutual fund. The loads and fees would be very high in the load international fund, so you're better off waiting for a few years until you have enough money to buy a good no-load international fund. For each fund we initially select, we'll collect information about its 1-year, 5-year, and 10-year returns, its fees, and its manager's tenure.

Let's assume you have $10,000 to set up this portfolio, which means we will put $5,000 into a growth stock fund, $2,500 into a value stock fund, $2,000 into long-term bond funds, and hold $500 in a cash account or money market fund.

As the portfolio grows, we can add an international fund at a later date when reallocating this portfolio.

We talk about reallocating and managing portfolios in the next chapter.

So let's start with a Growth fund. Using the Morningstar Star Mutual Fund Screener (http://screen.morningstar.com/FundSelector.html?fsection=ToolScreener), we set the fund group to domestic stock, set the category to large growth, minimum initial purchase equal to or less than $5,000, no-load funds only, and expense ratio less than or equal to 1 percent. We then score the results making 5-year and 10-year returns the highest priority, as well as making lowest fees a priority.

These three no-load growth stock mutual funds come out on top:

Mutual Fund	1 Year	3 Year	5 Year	10 Year	Fees	Management Tenure
Fidelity Contrafund	14.14	14.46	11.21	11.22	.91	1990
T. Rowe Price Growth Stock	15.66	10.85	6.9	9.33	.72	1997
Vanguard Morgan Growth	13.63	10.31	7.45	8.04	.39	1994

Mutual Fund	1 Year	3 Year	5 Year	10 Year	Fees	Management Tenure
Fidelity Contrafund	14.14	14.46	11.21	11.22	.91	1990
T. Rowe Price Growth Stock	15.66	10.85	6.9	9.33	.72	1997
Vanguard Morgan Growth	13.63	10.31	7.45	8.04	.39	1994

The fund with the best 10-year average annual return is the Fidelity Contrafund. Another good point this fund has going for it is that it has the manager with the longest tenure. You've got a better chance that the historical returns can be repeated with a manager that's been there a long time. We'll use Fidelity Contrafund for this practice portfolio.

If you were doing the search for yourself, before choosing any fund, you would, of course, need to read the prospectus to be sure the fund's investing strategy matches your own strategy. You also want to research information from independent analysts about this fund. We talk about how to research funds in Chapter 5.

Next, we'll find the value fund. We set the fund group to domestic stock, set the category to large value, minimum initial purchase equal to or less than $2,000, no-load funds only, and expense ratio less than or equal to 1 percent. I then score the results making 5-year and 10-year returns the highest priority, as well as lowest fees.

These two no-load value mutual funds come out on top:

Mutual Fund	1 Year	3 Year	5 Year	10 Year	Fees	Management Tenure
Vantagepoint Equity Income	16.12	14.23	10.2		.89	1999
Homestead Value	18.23	15.95	11.26	9.83	.76	1990

In this category, I found only two possibilities. Many of the no-load mutual funds require a higher initial investment than $2,500. Looking just at these numbers, Homestead Value looks the better of the two, so we'll use that fund for this practice portfolio.

Next, we find the bond fund. I set the fund group to taxable bond, set the category to large blend, minimum initial purchase equal to or less than $2,000, no-load funds only, and expense ratio less than or equal to 1 percent. We then score the results making 5-year and 10-year returns the highest priority, as well as lowest fees.

Three no-load bond mutual funds come out on top:

Mutual Fund	1 Year	3 Year	5 Year	10 Year	Fees	Management Tenure
PIA BBB Bond	2.17	3.16			.41	
Inflation Protected	0.95				.79	2004
Sextant Bond Income	2.11	2.75	4.78	6.46	.94	1994

The choices for no-load bond fund were not good. You really do need to have $3,000 to invest to get into one of the better index bond funds. Bond index funds are the best because the fees are low and you really don't need to pay for managed bond funds. If you have less than $3,000 to put into a bond fund, your best bet may be to find a money market account with a bank at a decent interest and wait until you have that much to invest. We will use Sextant Bond Income for this portfolio because it does have a decent 10-year track record.

Here is the Growth portfolio we just developed:

Mutual Fund	Investment	10-year average annual return	Percentage of Portfolio	Weighted Average Annual Return
Fidelity Contrafund	$5,000	11.22	.5	5.75
Homestead Value	$2,500	9.83	.25	2.46
Sextant Bond Income	$2,000	6.46	.2	1.29
Cash	$500	3.0	.05	0.15
Portfolio Total	$10,000			9.65

As you can see, the average annual return for this portfolio made up of actual mutual funds matches the historical average for the same type of portfolio discussed previously.

We do want to reiterate that this was a practice using the mutual fund screener tools and not a recommendation for the ideal portfolio. After you've screened out your possibilities, then request a prospectus from each of the companies and read them carefully. I talk about what you should look for in a prospectus in Chapter 3.

You also may want to consider getting a premium subscription with Morningstar if you plan to build your investment portfolio using mutual funds. By getting a premium subscription, you will be able to access Morningstar's excellent mutual fund analysis and do a better job of picking top funds. The annual subscription is $135 for one year, but you can try it out for free for two weeks.

Putting Your Portfolio on Autopilot

If you decide you really don't want to worry about constructing your portfolio at all, you can choose to use an asset allocation portfolio or a life strategy portfolio. Many mutual fund companies do offer those options, but you will pay higher fees for the management of these types of portfolios.

Many life strategy portfolios are set for a particular retirement year, such as 2015 or 2030. You pick the portfolio that comes closest to the year you plan to retire. The mutual fund company will then set your asset allocation to best meet your needs. For example, if you pick a life strategy portfolio for retirement in 2030, the initial phase of the portfolio would be allocated for more risk and better growth. As you get closer to 2030, the allocation would gradually shift to one that is more conservative to preserve principal.

These types of mutual funds are more expensive because you must pay two managers. One manager picks the mutual funds for the portfolio, and another person manages the actual assets in each mutual fund portfolio picked for the life strategy portfolio.

In the next chapter, we explore how to manage a portfolio after you've made your selections.

The Least You Need to Know

- Know your goals, your investment horizon, and your risk tolerance before deciding on a portfolio mix.

- Don't invest using a riskier portfolio than you can tolerate, or you will end up getting nervous and selling the portfolio when the market is down, which will likely result in your losing a significant amount of money.

- You can put your portfolio on autopilot if you don't want to worry about constructing one yourself, but you will pay significantly higher fees.

Chapter

Managing Your Portfolio

In This Chapter

- Watch over your investments
- Considering changes
- Study your statements

Do you wish you could just take the time to do all the initial research, pick your mutual funds, and then just let the entire portfolio run on autopilot? Many of us may wish we could do this. Wouldn't it be nice if investing were that simple? But, unfortunately, it's not.

Unless you decide to pay the extra fees and have someone else manage your portfolio for you (such as through a life strategy mutual fund or by hiring a financial advisor), you need to monitor what is happening with your investment choices, as well as watch to be sure your asset allocation is remaining within your level of risk tolerance.

In this chapter, we discuss how you can do that and what steps you should take after you construct your portfolio.

Monitoring Your Investments

Sometimes you may think the business press covers the stock market like it's a sports game. You can turn on almost any cable news station and get at least 10 minutes every hour reporting the ups and downs of the stock market almost as a sportscaster reports the innings of a baseball game.

You can get caught up in all that hype and think you must run and shift your portfolio to match the day's news, but don't get caught up in all the hype and respond too quickly to a bad news day. Remember you are investing for the long term, not to sell your assets in the next few days, weeks, or months. You have the time to ride out any immediate storm.

Whenever you think about making a change to your portfolio, do it with careful consideration of why you initially picked the investment and what has changed that is making you want to reconsider your choice.

Planning Periodic Reviews

Your best bet, especially if you find listening to the daily business chatter nerve-wracking, is to set up definite times during the year when you actually plan to review your portfolio, test your asset allocation, and review the performance of all the funds you've chosen. You should only plan to make changes necessary after that careful review.

Unless you're facing a dramatic life change, such as getting married, getting divorced, or facing the death of a family member, a good plan is to analyze your portfolio every six months. Then make any needed changes after that planned review. That should be frequent enough to keep your portfolio on track.

Reacting to Bad News

Don't jump quickly when you hear bad news about the stock or bond market. The only news that will be important to you is the news about a change of managers for a mutual fund in your portfolio. Sometimes a manager change is good for a portfolio, especially if you've been seeing a gradual decline in the results, and sometimes it can be very bad news.

For example, if a fund manager has been with the fund for years and suddenly decides to leave even though the fund is doing well, that can be a bad sign. The new manager may not bring the same level of skills to the portfolio, and the performance could suffer.

If you find the new manager worked under the former manager for many years, you definitely should give the new manager some time and watch what he does. Many times in this type of scenario, the new manager has been well trained by his mentor and will continue to manage the mutual fund portfolio in the same way, so you have no reason to panic.

If the new manager is totally new to the fund, you need to research what the manager has done in the past. The mutual fund company should be able to get you some background information about the new manager. You also will probably see stories written by mutual fund analysts on websites such as Morningstar (www.morningstar.com) or Marketwatch (www.marketwatch.com). Both websites do an excellent job of covering major changes in the mutual fund industry.

Another good website to watch is Fund Alarm (www.fundalarm.com), which reports monthly on all mutual fund manager changes. You can even set up to get a free e-mail reminder to alert you that the site has put out a new report.

Whether you are doing a planned periodic review or beginning a review after hearing mutual funds news that disturbed you, don't jump quickly to make changes to your portfolio. Remember a mutual fund portfolio is made up of lots of different stocks or bonds, and it will take a long time for a new manager to make changes to the portfolio that could dramatically impact its performance.

If the performance of any of your mutual funds is negative, that doesn't automatically mean you need to pick something else. You should research the performance of other similar mutual funds and determine how well your fund is doing compared to similar funds. You may find that the performance of your fund, while not great, is better than other funds of the same type.

You can compare performance of your fund to other similar funds very simply by going to Morningstar and searching for your fund. After putting its name in the quote search box, you should be linked directly to the fund's snapshot page or a list of possible choices. If you get a list of mutual fund choices, click on the link that will take you to the fund's snapshot page.

For example, here is the link to the snapshot page for one of the largest and most popular index funds, Vanguard 500 Index——http://quicktake. morningstar.com/Fund/Snapshot.asp?Country =USA&Symbol=VFINX. If you have a hard time using this rather long link, go to the opening page of Morningstar.com and put in VFINX (the symbol for the fund) into the "quotes" box on the top left of the page.

When you get to that page you'll see a performance chart, and below that chart you'll see the performance results for the fund and comparison lines showing you how the fund is doing compared to other funds in the category, as well as how it is doing compared to the Standard & Poor's index. You can get even more detail about performance by clicking on total returns in the left column. There you can get a long-term history with the same performance comparisons. After looking at those comparisons, you can see whether your fund is doing better or worse than other funds in the same category.

Never focus only on short-term results. Remember you are investing for the long term, so don't jump out of the fund if the only negative performance is in the past quarter or year. All funds go up and down through good and bad times. Yes, even mutual fund mangers make mistakes picking stocks or bonds, and the performance of the portfolio will suffer. Sometimes a couple of bad picks, such as the choice of industry, can be a major drag on short-term performance, but the manager may be looking at a long-term recovery for the industry involved and expect major gain just around the corner. So don't sell your mutual fund just because it's down for the short term, rather research to find out why.

Reading an analyst's report about the fund will help you to understand the strategy and whether the fund's downturn is expected to be short-term because of market conditions or long-term because of a manager change that is not working. If you have Morningstar's premium service, which we do recommend you at least try for free for two weeks (it costs $135 per year), you can click on the link to the left of the page called "Analyst Research." You will quickly find out what the analyst thinks about the fund. In addition to the most recent analyst report, you will also find a link to an analyst report archive, so you can read past reports as well.

You can also search the Internet for additional stories about your mutual fund and find out what other analysts are saying about the fund. If you do find that many analysts agree the fund is heading for bad news, then start your research to find another fund that better matches your goals. Move slowly and deliberately to make a change. Don't jump into some other investment in panic.

Mutual funds are not like stocks. They don't drop dramatically in price because of bad news about the fund, but mutual funds can drop dramatically in price if the entire market collapses on bad news, as happened after the Internet bubble burst in 2001 and most stocks on the market dropped in value. No stock mutual fund was immune to loss during that period, but some did lose less than others.

Fund Fears

Don't lock in a loss by selling mutual funds when most of the stock market is down. That definitely is not a time to sell. There is no reason to lock in that type of loss. You should ride out the storm if the market takes a major nosedive like that.

After the Internet bubble burst, many of the mutual funds that focused primarily on growth, especially high-tech companies, lost 60 to 80 percent of their value because the underlying stocks they held all lost market value. These were primarily technology sector mutual funds or aggressive growth funds.

Fund Fears

If you do decide to add sector funds or aggressive growth funds to your portfolio, only do so when you are ready to monitor your portfolio more frequently, as well as monitor the market more closely. You also should be able to tolerate a lot of risk and not make hasty moves based on a bad news day.

Reallocating Your Portfolio

Whether you decide to make a change to your portfolio based on mutual fund news or because of a change after a major life event, always test your asset allocation first and see if it's still in line with the asset allocation you initially planned.

Suppose you decided on a moderate portfolio, similar to this moderate portfolio we discussed in Chapter 7:

- Stock Funds   **60 percent**
     Growth stock funds   30 percent
     Value stock funds   30 percent
- Bond Mutual Funds   **30 percent**
     Intermediate-term bond funds   15 percent
     Long-term bond funds   15 percent
- Cash/Money Market Funds   **10 percent**

Suppose you picked funds in each of these categories and now want to see if the portfolio still matches your initial asset allocation. Pull together all your most current mutual fund statements, which will show how many shares you own and the value of each fund as of the date of that report. To be sure you are looking at the most current market data, go to Morningstar and look for the most recent share price. Then multiply that share price times the number of shares you hold to find the current market value for your holdings.

For example, suppose you own 100 shares of Fund A, which closed at a *Net Asset Value (NAV)* of $45.

To calculate the market value, multiply 100 times $45. In this scenario, the current market value is $4,500.

def•i•ni•tion

Net Asset Value (NAV) is the dollar value of a single mutual fund share. The value is calculated based on the value of all the assets held in the mutual fund minus any liabilities and then divided by the number of shares outstanding. The NAV is calculated after market close each business day.

After you calculate the market value for all your holdings, enter the date into a worksheet with three columns, one for the mutual fund name, one for the market value, and one for the percentage of the portfolio. Just to give you an idea of what the worksheet might look like, here is the market value for a sample portfolio:

Name of Mutual Fund	Market Value	Percentage of Portfolio
ABC Growth Stock Fund	$5,000	39 percent
DEF Value Stock Fund	$3,500	27 percent
GHI Intermediate-term Bond Fund	$1,600	12 percent
JKL Long-term Bond Fund	$1,700	13 percent

continues

continued

Name of Mutual Fund	Market Value	Percentage of Portfolio
Cash	$1,100	9 percent
Total	$12,900	

As you can see, the asset allocation no longer matches the allocation for a conservative portfolio. The growth stock fund did very well and now represents a much larger share of the portfolio than you initially planned. You now have a greater exposure to growth stocks than you might want.

The portfolio could look very different if it was a bad year for stocks and a good year for bonds. If after your periodic review you find your asset allocation out of whack, you can do one of two things to adjust your portfolio:

- Invest a lump sum of any new investments in the type of mutual funds assets that are below your intended allocation targets.
- Reallocate your assets by selling the mutual fund types that exceed your target allocation and buying the mutual fund types that are below the allocation you want.

If you do decide to sell your assets in one fund and buy another, you may be subject to taxes on any gains you made while you held the mutual fund. We talk more about the tax impacts on mutual fund buying and selling decisions in Chapter 9.

Don't think you always have to keep your asset allocation perfectly proportioned. Each time you do a periodic review of your portfolio, you will find that the allocation is out of whack. Your best bet is to just buy additional shares in the types of mutual funds that are low and gradually get yourself back to your asset allocation.

If you find that the asset allocation is so out of whack that you'll never be able to catch up, you might then want to sell some shares of the mutual fund doing very well and buy shares of one that is growing more slowly. Remember, bond funds will usually grow at a slower rate than stock funds unless it's a very bad year for stocks.

The reason many mutual fund shareholders were hurt during the stock crash of 2001 is that they lost track of the importance of asset allocation as the Internet stock bubble got larger and larger. Rather than reallocate their portfolios to sell some of their shares in growth mutual funds and preserve their profits, they got greedy and just watched them grow. When the bubble finally burst, their portfolios dropped below the amount that they initially invested in the funds. Those who kept buying the growth funds to take advantage of the bubble lost even more because they bought shares at higher and higher prices.

You'll find it hard not to jump on the bandwagon when you see the stock market soaring higher and higher, but you'll be happy you didn't when the stock market corrects itself, which it always does. You may find it even harder to sell holdings in a mutual fund that is doing extremely well, but it's a good idea to maintain your asset allocation and not get caught up in market hype.

 Fund Fears

Investors couldn't wait to buy the Internet Fund in 2000—today called Kinetics Internet (WWWFX). In 1999 the fund soared to 216.4 percent. Now doesn't that sound great? Hold your horses. In 2000 the fund lost 51.5 percent. It lost 9.6 percent in 2001 and 23.4 percent in 2002. If you were one of the unlucky investors who bought the fund in March 2000 at the height of the stock bubble, you'd still be looking at a loss of money. The fund finally started to turn around in 2003 with a gain of 40.1 percent, but after three years of losses totaling 84.5 percent you would still be sitting in a loss position today. Investors who bought this mutual fund at the high of $61.54 in March 2000 could only sell the fund for $28.71 in December 2006. Minimal dividends ranging from $.005 to $.366 per share have been paid yearly.

You could make a conscious decision that you feel more comfortable about your investing skills. You may also be able to tolerate more risk as your confidence builds. You could decide to shift to a different asset allocation that allows you to put a greater percentage of your portfolio into stocks.

There's nothing wrong with making the decision to shift your asset allocation as long as you make it carefully and know you can live with it and still sleep at night. Your biggest danger will be to take on too much risk and run to sell your holdings at a loss when the market drops.

Another good investing strategy for mutual funds is called dollar cost averaging. When using this strategy, a prudent investor will decide to invest a set amount every month no matter what that market is doing.

 Mutual Aids

> One good way to steadily increase your portfolio is dollar cost averaging. With this method of investing, you add to your portfolio on a set schedule. Your money will buy more shares when the price is lower and fewer shares when the price is higher. Over time you will find that this method has enabled you to have a lower average cost per share then someone who only buys shares when he hears good news about the fund.

Reading Your Mutual Fund Statements

Your mutual fund companies will send you semi-annual reports every six months. They're required to do that. Many mutual fund companies even send reports quarterly for all the funds where you hold shares. If you decide to invest using a mutual fund supermarket or broker, then you will get these statements from the company that holds your mutual fund shares.

Don't just look at the bottom line and get excited if your portfolio goes up or disappointed if your portfolio goes down. Don't just take a quick look and throw them away. Spend some time reviewing the types of stocks and bonds included in the portfolio, and maybe research some of the companies yourself if you don't recognize them.

If you have some questions about the investment strategy, do some additional digging to find out what others are saying about the fund. One great website to find out more about management changes and other problem alarms is FundAlarm. com. You can sign up for a free monthly e-mail that lets you know when the site is updated.

Also take the time to read the statement from the mutual fund portfolio manager regarding the fund's results and what he anticipates for the fund in the future. Monitor that information for indications that the mutual fund manager may be planning significant changes in the way the fund is managed or the fund's investment strategy.

You will have the opportunity to vote on any major strategy changes that differ from what were stated in the mutual fund prospectus when you bought the fund. If you don't like the changes because the fund's investment objectives will no longer match your own investment strategy, it's a good time to think about selling the mutual fund and buying a new one. For example, if you are a conservative investor and find that the mutual fund manager wants to start investing in riskier assets, you may want to find a different fund.

If you find out by reading the statement that there is a major management change for one of your mutual fund picks, don't panic. Unlike a stock that is hit with bad news and can drop dramatically in a day, mutual funds take longer to show the effects of a manager change. Even if the manager plans to make a major shift in mutual fund strategy, it usually takes months, or sometimes even years, to buy and sell assets strategically.

Just because a fund changes managers does not automatically mean you should sell it. Research the new manager's performance. Most likely he or she managed at least one other fund before taking over yours. Websites like FundAlarm.com, Morningstar.com and Marketwatch do cover manager changes and will frequently give you a good deal of information about whether the change is good or bad for the fund.

The Least You Need to Know

- After constructing your mutual fund portfolio, you can't just put it on hold; you must plan a regular schedule for monitoring your portfolio.

- Don't make changes in your portfolio based on a bad news day. Always take time to research your fund to see how it is doing compared to other similar funds.

- A change in mutual fund managers can be bad news and should be researched, but don't jump quickly to change mutual funds. They won't drop quickly in a day when bad news is reported as an individual stock can.

Taxes and Your Mutual Funds

In This Chapter

- Capital gains
- Dividends
- Interest
- Deferrals

Reporting dividends and capital gains is much more complicated for mutual funds than it is for stocks. Even if you reinvest all your earnings on your mutual funds, you'll still need to pay taxes on most of the dividends and capital gains that you earn, unless your funds are inside a tax-deferred or tax-free retirement portfolio.

In this chapter, we review the various rules regarding mutual funds, taxes, and the gains you get from your mutual funds.

Outside a Retirement Portfolio

Let's start with the rules for mutual funds you hold outside a qualified retirement portfolio, such as a

401(k) or IRA. The rules are different for mutual funds held inside a qualified retirement portfolio, and we discuss those below.

When you hold mutual fund shares, you will likely get certain gains each year including dividends and capital gains. You must report each even if you never receive the cash because you reinvest the money into additional shares of the mutual fund.

Capital Gains

You may get three different types of capital gains distributions from a mutual fund, including:

- Long-term capital gains, also called long-term capital dividends, are gains on assets held more than 12 months. You must report these gains even if you reinvested the money. If you are in the 15 percent tax bracket or lower, these capital gains will be taxed at a rate of 5 percent. If you are in a higher tax bracket, these capital gains will be taxed at 15 percent.

- Short-term capital gains, gains earned on assets held less than one year, are taxed at your current income tax rate. These are profits on the sale of assets held for less than one year.

- Undistributed long-term capital gains, which are also called capital gain allocations, are capital gains that are held by the mutual fund rather than being paid out to the shareholders.

How do you know which type of capital gains distribution you receive and what to do with the information at tax time? If the form you receive the information on is a 1099-DIV, you will find capital gain distributions in Box 2A. You should report them along with any other capital gains distributions on your Schedule D. You can see what a 1099-DIV looks like in Figure 09-01.

When your mutual fund pays the taxes on the capital gains, the company will send you a special statement called the "Notice to Shareholder of Undistributed Long-Term Gains" (Form 2439). This form can arrive a month later than your 1099-DIV because mutual fund companies have 60 days to prepare this form, while they must send the 1099-DIV by January 31 of the next year.

If you do receive a Form 2439, you have to report the capital gains on your income tax return as you would other long-term capital gains, but in addition you can claim a credit for any tax paid by the mutual fund company. This credit will be shown on Form 2439. If you get a Form 2439, you will get a copy that you can attach to your tax return.

In addition to reporting gains on your tax returns, you also need to keep track of all reinvested capital gains and dividends or undistributed capital gains so you can add this to your basis (the cost of initially buying the mutual fund). It's important to keep track of these gains because you can add their value to the cost of purchasing the mutual fund when you sell it. Since you've already paid tax on this money, you won't pay tax on it again. This will reduce any long-term capital gains you must pay at the time you sell the fund.

Sample of a 1099-DIV statement used for reporting capital gains and dividends from your mutual funds.

☐ CORRECTED (if checked)

PAYER'S name, street address, city, state, ZIP code, and telephone no.	1a Total ordinary dividends $	OMB No. 1545-0110 2006 Form 1099-DIV	Dividends and Distributions
	1b Qualified dividends $		Copy B For Recipient
	2a Total capital gain distr. $	2b Unrecap. Sec. 1250 gain $	
PAYER'S federal identification number	RECIPIENT'S identification number		
RECIPIENT'S name	2c Section 1202 gain $	2d Collectibles (28%) gain $	This is important tax information and is being furnished to the Internal Revenue Service. If you are required to file a return, a negligence penalty or other sanction may be imposed on you if this income is taxable and the IRS determines that it has not been reported.
	3 Nondividend distributions $	4 Federal income tax withheld $	
Street address (including apt. no.)		5 Investment expenses $	
City, state, and ZIP code	6 Foreign tax paid $	7 Foreign country or U.S. possession	
Account number (see instructions)	8 Cash liquidation distributions $	9 Noncash liquidation distributions $	

Form **1099-DIV**   (keep for your records)   Department of the Treasury - Internal Revenue Service

VOID	CORRECTED	(99)	

| OMB No. 1545-0145 | | **Notice to Shareholder of Undistributed Long-Term Capital Gains** | |

Name, address, and ZIP code of RIC or REIT

2005

Form **2439**

For calendar year 2005, or other tax year of the regulated investment company (RIC) or the real estate investment trust (REIT)

beginning .... , 2005, and

ending .... 20 ......

Copy A

Attach to
Form 1120-RIC
or Form 1120-REIT

1a Total undistributed long-term capital gains	

Identification number of RIC or REIT

1b Unrecaptured section 1250 gain	

Shareholder's identifying number

1c Section 1202 gain	1d Collectibles (28%) gain

Shareholder's name, address, and ZIP code

2 Tax paid by the RIC or REIT on the box 1a gains	

For Instructions and Paperwork Reduction Act Notice, see back of Copies A and D.

Form **2439**	Cat. No. 11858E	Department of the Treasury - Internal Revenue Service

Sample of the Form 2439 used for reporting undistributed long-term capital gains from your mutual funds.

Your best bet is to keep a file of all mutual fund annual statements so you'll have a good history of all the capital gains on which you already paid taxes. We talk more about tax basis and how to calculate taxes on gains when you sell mutual funds below.

Dividends

Look for two different types of dividends when you get your 1099-DIV from the mutual fund. They are:

- Qualified dividends are ordinary dividends that are taxed at the rate of 5 percent if you are in the 10 percent or 15 percent tax bracket and at 15 percent for all other tax payers.
- Nonqualified dividends are ordinary dividends that are taxed at your regular income tax rates.

You can tell whether you get qualified or nonqualified dividends by looking at the 1099-DIV. Total ordinary dividends are on line 1A and qualified dividends are on line 1B. Line 1A does include both types of dividends. When you fill out your tax return, you'll see a place to put ordinary dividends when reporting your income on the Form 1040. Use the information on line 1A for that. Then you'll see a special line below that line for ordinary dividends on the 1040 to report qualified dividends. Use the information on Line 1B for that.

For example, if Line 1A indicates $300 and Line 1B indicates $200, then you have received a total of

$300 in dividends, but $200 of them were qualified for the lower tax rates. Follow the instructions in the 1040 for calculating taxes on your dividends.

What are the nonqualified dividends? They can be one of three types of payouts:

- **Taxable interest**   If a mutual fund earns interest on its assets, it is paid out to shareholders as a dividend. But since the money earned did not get paid into the mutual fund as a dividend, it gets paid out as unqualified dividends.

- **Nonqualified dividends**   Sometimes a mutual fund will receive a dividend that did not qualify for the lower tax rate. When this happens, the fund must report it as a nonqualified dividend.

- **Short-term capital gains**   If the mutual fund had short-term capital gains during the year, these are reported as a nonqualified dividend.

Exempt Distributions

If you hold tax-exempt mutual funds, which are mutual funds whose assets include municipal bond funds and other nontaxable assets, then some, if not all, of the dividends will be exempt from federal taxation. You may have to pay state taxes on the interest dividends depending on the tax laws in your state.

Even if you hold a tax-exempt mutual fund, you may still end up with a taxable distribution of capital gains. Tax-exempt mutual funds will report gains or losses on the sale of their assets.

Foreign Taxes

If you own international mutual funds, you may get a statement indicating that the mutual fund paid foreign taxes. This will be shown on Line 6 of the 1099-DIV.

If you itemize deductions, you can claim this amount on Schedule A when you file your taxes. List this on line 8 (other taxes) and call it "foreign tax from 1099-DIV."

This is the simplest way to handle any foreign taxes paid, but if you find you paid a significant amount in foreign taxes, you may want to consider filing for the Foreign Tax Credit. You can read more about this complicated process at www.irs.gov/pub/irs-pdf/p514.pdf.

Inside a Retirement Portfolio

If you hold your mutual funds inside a qualified retirement portfolio, you don't need to worry about your annual statements reporting capital gains and dividend distributions. You will pay taxes on these gains when you start withdrawing the money in retirement.

Mutual Aids

Remember most qualified retirement plans are tax-deferred. All mutual funds withdrawn from an employer-sponsored qualified retirement account (401(k), 403(b), SEP-IRA, SIMPLE IRA, KEOGH), or a traditional individual retirement account (IRA) will only be taxed when you start drawing down the funds after the age of 59½. If you start taking out the money before you reach age 59½, you may also have to pay penalties on the withdrawal.

You may never have to pay taxes at all on these capital gains and dividends if you hold your mutual funds in Roth IRAs. Any money withdrawn from a Roth IRA in retirement is withdrawn tax free as long as you've had the account for five years or more and are at least 59½.

Taxes When Selling Mutual Funds

Another time you must worry about taxes is when it comes time to sell your mutual funds that are held outside a retirement portfolio. Sales or exchanges of funds inside a retirement portfolio are tax-deferred, as long as you buy another mutual fund or other asset and keep it within the retirement portfolio.

Any time you withdraw money from a mutual fund, you are actually selling shares of stock in that mutual fund. You must report a sale of mutual funds in much the same way as you would report a stock sale, but the cost basis for the mutual fund can be a bit more complex to figure out.

Selling mutual fund shares and calculating the taxes on any capital gains can be a relatively easy thing to figure out if you bought all the shares on one day and sold the same shares at some time in the future. If you held the shares for at least 12 months, you would calculate the gain the same way you would for any long-term capital gain. If you held the shares of the mutual fund for less than 12 months, then you would calculate the gain as you would for a short-term capital gain.

You figure out a capital gain by subtracting what you paid for the asset from what you sold the asset. If the difference is positive, it means you made money on the transaction or you had a capital gain. If the answer is negative, it means you lost money on the transaction and you suffered a capital loss.

For example, suppose you bought 100 shares of the mutual fund at $10 a share for a total cost basis of $1,000. Then you sold the 100 shares for $15 for a total of $1,500. Subtract $1,000 from $1,500, and you get a positive number of $500. That means you had a $500 capital gain. If you held the shares for more than 12 months, it would be a $500 long-term capital gain and would be taxed at 5 percent if you are in the 10 or 15 percent tax bracket and 15 percent if you are in a tax bracket above 15 percent. If you held the shares for less than 12 months, then it would be a short-term capital gain, and you would be taxed at your current income tax rate on the gain.

Suppose we reverse this example, and you paid $1,500 to buy the shares of the mutual fund and sold them for $1,000. When you subtract $1,500 from $1,000, you get a negative number, which means you suffered a $500 capital loss. You can use capital losses to write down capital gains on Schedule D when you file your tax returns.

While this may seem like a relatively easy calculation, it's rare that you own exactly the same number of shares on the day you bought the mutual fund as you do on the day you sell the fund. It's even more rare that the shares will sell for the exact same amount as the time you bought them.

Most people reinvest their capital gains and dividends distributions and buy additional shares during the time they own the fund. Many also buy additional shares while they hold the fund. For example, you may invest $100 a month after your initial purchase. You likely bought the additional shares at a different share price each time.

When you start to withdraw money from the fund at retirement, you likely won't sell your entire holdings all at once. That, too, can make it complicated to figure out the taxes you owe. You likely would sell the shares at a different price each time as well.

How does all this impact the amount you have to pay in taxes on the gain from a mutual fund sale? Well, that depends on the price you receive when you sell the shares. It also depends on the method you use to calculate the cost basis of the shares. You can use FIFO, specific identification of shares, or averaging. Let's take a look at each of these options for calculating cost basis.

Regular IRS Rules or FIFO

If you don't tell the IRS something different, it will assume that you used its regular rules of FIFO (First In, First Out). These state that the shares you bought first are the ones that are sold first. The IRS will expect you to use the price for the oldest shares as the cost basis for calculating your capital gains. Many times the shares bought the earliest are also the lowest price shares, so when you subtract the amount received after sale, you'll end up with the highest possible capital gains.

For example, suppose at the time of your initial purchase you paid $10 a share for 100 shares or $1,000. Then you continued buying $100 worth of additional shares every month. You bought some of these shares for $11, some for $12, and on upwards throughout the time period you owned the mutual fund. When you decide it's time to sell some shares, the share price is $20 per share. Your most recent purchase of shares was at $18 per share.

If you use the FIFO method when selling 100 shares, the cost basis for these shares was $1,000, so the capital gains when sold at $20 per share would be $10 per share. You can reduce this by identifying specific shares.

Identify Specific Shares

You can identify the specific shares you are selling and use the purchase price of those sales as your cost basis provided you do that in writing before you make the sale. For example, when you give the instructions to sell the shares, you must indicate in your instructions which specific shares you are selling, such as the most recent shares you bought at such and such a price. Your broker or mutual fund company would have to send back a confirmation of this instruction before selling the shares.

As long as you have all this in writing, you can then use the cost basis of the shares you designated you were selling. You can minimize the capital gains hit by designating the higher-priced shares as the ones sold. If you do choose this method, keep very careful records of what shares you have and what shares you sell. You can't sell the same priced shares twice.

 Mutual Aids

> If you do use the specific identification method when selling shares, all you are doing is delaying the inevitable. Eventually you will have to pay the capital gains on the oldest shares, but you can plan that for a year when your income is lower so the tax rate may not be as high.

Averaging Method

You may find the averaging method a simpler way to track your sales than the specific identification method, but it will result in a lower capital gains hit than the FIFO method. You total the amount you contributed plus add any reinvested capital gains or dividends to find your cost basis. Remember you've already paid tax on the reinvested capital gains and dividends, so you don't want to be taxed twice.

Once you get that total, divide the total value of your contributions and reinvestments by the total number of mutual fund shares you hold. This will give you an average cost basis per share.

You can actually choose from two averaging methods when calculating the average cost basis:

- **Single-Category Method**   This is the easier of the two and all shares are calculated under one method. When you use the single category method for average cost basis, you assume the first shares are sold first. That's a good thing because you want to sell shares you've held the longest hoping that all shares will fall under the long-term capital gains tax rules rather than short-term capital gains tax rules.

- **Double-Category Method**   This method is more complex and separates shares held for the long-term and shares held less than 12 months. You would calculate an average cost basis separately for the long-term shares and the short-term shares. Then you can designate which shares you sold.

Initially the averaging methods may seem very complex, but once you've done the initial calculations and learn how to use these methods, you will quickly see the advantage of averaging.

You can learn more about the tax rules impacting mutual funds by reading IRS Publication 564 (www.irs.gov/publications/p564/index.html), "Mutual Fund Distributions."

The Least You Need to Know

- You must pay taxes on capital gains and dividends for all mutual funds held outside a retirement account even if you reinvest the money and don't take out any cash.

- Taxes are deferred until you withdraw the money at retirement on most gains for mutual funds held within a qualified retirement account. The only exception is for mutual funds held in a Roth IRA, which grow tax-free. You may pay penalties if you withdraw funds from a retirement account before the age of 59½.

- You can calculate the cost basis for a mutual fund by using three methods—FIFO, specific identification, or averaging.

Chapter 10

Fixing Fund Problems

In This Chapter

- Purchasing worries
- Acknowledging receipt
- Transferring funds
- Opting to do things differently
- Locating lost funds

Stuff happens and sometimes things will go wrong with your mutual fund accounts. In this chapter, we review the common problems mutual fund shareholders encounter and how to deal with them.

Deposit or Purchase Errors

Everyone makes mistakes. You may occasionally end up with your purchase being made to the wrong mutual fund within a fund family. So many mutual funds have similar names that this can and does happen.

Always look at your purchase confirmation as soon as it arrives in the mail and be certain it matches what you intended to do. If your mutual fund account is available online, you can check it even sooner by logging into your account the day after you made arrangements for your purchase.

If you find an error, call the mutual fund company as soon as possible and talk with one of its customer service people. If the mistake was the fault of the mutual fund company, they should be more than happy to try to resolve the issue for you. You will need a copy of your instructions to the mutual fund to prove the error.

The company should reverse the purchase based on the price you paid for the funds and permit you to purchase the funds at the share price you would have gotten if the purchase had been processed correctly. If the customer service person can't help you do things this way, then ask to talk with a supervisor.

 Fund Fears

Always double-check all your information before beginning any transaction with your mutual fund company. If you frequently request changes in your transactions, the mutual fund company will be less and less willing to help you correct errors without charging redemption or other transaction fees.

If you gave the wrong orders to the mutual fund company when you made the purchase, own up to your mistake. As long as it's not something you do frequently, the customer service person will likely be able to work with you to correct the purchase order.

You likely will not be able to reverse the purchase and get the fund you intended at the price available on the day of your original transaction, but if there are any transaction fees for redemption, you may be able to get those fees waived. Sometimes if you aren't able to get the help you want the first time, it's worth calling again. You most likely will get a different customer service person and the second person may be more willing to help. You can always ask for a supervisor if the person on the line is not being helpful.

Many mutual fund companies do permit you to buy, exchange, or sell funds using their online systems. You may find that it's easier to manage the transaction completely on your own, or you may prefer to work with an individual to handle your transactions. Whichever way works well for you is the one you should choose.

Verifying Receipt of Your Money

It's always a good idea to verify that the mutual fund company received your money and used it to purchase the correct mutual fund shares. How quickly you should do that depends on how you made the purchase. Today you can purchase shares by mail, by telephone, in person, by Internet transaction, and by wire. The following explains how you should verify each purchase method.

- **Purchase by mail** If you haven't received something confirming your transaction in writing a week after you sent the check, you can call your mutual fund company and verify that it was received. Be sure you write a letter with clear instructions regarding what you want done with the money. While on the phone, also verify which shares they purchased. Eventually you will get something in writing, but sometimes that can take a few weeks. It's best to check receipt as soon as possible. That way if there is a problem, you can correct it quickly before too much time has passed making the solution more difficult.

- **Purchase by telephone** If you're set up for purchase by telephone, you can call your mutual fund company and make arrangements to purchase additional shares by electronic transfer from the bank account you've specified. After you see the money is taken out of your bank account, then call to verify that they received it and used it to purchase the correct mutual fund shares. Purchase by telephone is an option you can set up when you first open the account or ask to change to that option at a later date. If you don't have telephone transfer set up and you want to establish it, call your mutual fund company to find out how to arrange for it.

- **Purchase in person** If you opened your account through a broker or mutual fund supermarket (such as Charles Schwab), you may have an office for the firm near your home and decide to walk in and give them a check. Just to be on the safe side, call the broker a few days later to be sure he has purchased the correct mutual fund shares. Brokers can make a mistake or a check can be lost, and it's always a good idea to check things out quickly so he can more easily rectify a mistake.

- **Purchase by Internet** Many mutual fund companies have websites that are set up to handle mutual fund transactions online. When you first set up your account, you can opt to use electronic transfer of funds and set up for a link between the mutual fund company and your bank account. You will then be able to buy and sell mutual funds and have the money transferred between the mutual fund and your personal bank account. If you do decide to handle your transactions by Internet, you'll be able to access your account online the next business day and check to be sure the transaction was completed correctly and successfully. Most mutual companies will also send an e-mail confirmation of the transaction if you set up for that service.

- **Wire transfer** You can work with your bank to set up a wire transfer from your personal bank account into the mutual fund. You will need to write out specific instructions for how you want the money used. In most cases you will need to alert your mutual fund company about the transaction and specify what you want done with the funds when they arrive unless you have a standing order for dispersal of wire transfers. You will usually have to pay fees on both sides—to your bank and to your mutual fund company—to do transactions by wire. You're probably better off setting up electronic transfer if you plan to do this regularly.

Managing Fund Transfers

You may decide you want to move your funds from one mutual fund company to another. The easiest way to get such a transfer started is to contact the mutual fund company whose shares you want to buy. Set up an account with that company, and let them handle the transfer for you. Mutual fund companies have a standard set of forms for transferring funds.

When transferring or redeeming funds, you will likely need to get what is called a bank *signature guarantee*. The mutual fund company wants to be sure of your identity and your right to funds. You can take the signature guarantee form to your bank, and a customer service person there will verify your identity.

If you are transferring mutual funds that are held within a retirement portfolio, be sure to use a direct transfer method. You can end up paying penalties if the transfer of funds within an IRA is not handled correctly. While the law does give you 60 days to redeposit the money before penalties are due, you're much better off just letting the money transfer without having touched it. If not, you could be stuck having to prove to the Internal Revenue Service how and when the money moved out of one account and into another account within the 60-day window.

def•i•ni•tion

Signature guarantees, where you go to your bank to have your identity verified, are required for many securities transactions. This is both for your protection and the protection of the company handling the securities transactions. Signature guarantees make it harder for people to take your money by forging your signature on your securities certificates or related documents.

Sometimes you may find that your old mutual fund company or broker is reluctant to let go of your money. By law they must complete a transfer of funds in 30 days. If your transfer is not completed on time, call the old mutual fund company and find out why there is a delay. Keep pushing to talk with a manager if you don't get satisfaction from a customer service person.

If you have absolutely no luck getting the old mutual fund company to take action and release your funds, let them know that you're next contact will be to file a complaint with the National

Association of Securities Dealers or the Securities and Exchange Commission or both. In most cases that will get them to act quickly. No mutual fund wants to be part of an investigation by one of these U.S. government agencies. Hopefully, just the threat will get them to finish your transfer of funds quickly.

But you may need to carry through with your threat. You can file a complaint online with the SEC at https://tts.sec.gov/acts-ics/do/complaint. Or you can find the investor complaint center for the NASD at www.nasd.com/InvestorInformation/ InvestorProtection/InvestorComplaintCenter/ index.htm. If you have trouble using this link, go to www.nasd.com and click on the link to Investor Complaint Center. You'll find it on the front page of the website in the right column titled "Investor Information."

In some situations, you may find that you have to liquidate the funds first before you can transfer them. This can happen if you purchased mutual funds through a broker and the broker whose name is on the funds must first liquidate them for you. Yes, this can be a big hassle, but hold your ground and get the funds liquidated and ready for transfer. If you have problems, then contact the NASD or the SEC or both.

Changing Account Options

When you first open an account with a mutual fund, you pick many different options including how your additional purchases will be handled, who your beneficiaries will be, how you want your dividends and capital gains to be handled, whether or not you want to set up automatic investment options, and whether or not you want check-writing privileges (if they are available for the funds you have).

You'll answer a slew of questions on the mutual fund account application regarding these issues. However, the information you send to the mutual fund company is not set in stone. Changes to account options, such as reinvestment of dividends or purchases, you can usually do by telephone or by logging into your Internet account.

Other more significant changes, such as a change in name after you've been married or divorced, an address change, or a beneficiary change, can only be changed by writing to the mutual fund company. Often for a name change you will be required to get a bank signature guarantee.

If you do want to change your options, your best bet is to call the mutual fund company's customer service line first, explain the situation, and find out exactly what you need to do to make the change happen. Sometimes the company will need to send you a form that you must fill out, and other times they may just ask that you make the request by sending a letter stating the changes you want.

Calling first can save you time and frustration. You'll be able to do exactly what you need to do rather than spin your wheels and still not have the correction made.

Finding Lost Funds

Did you invest in mutual funds a long time ago and forget the details? Sometimes if you move around a lot, the mutual fund company will no longer be able to find you.

After sending numerous letters to your old address with no response, the mutual fund company does have the right to give up and mark your account as dormant. They will not send out any more statements for a number of years and eventually will consider your account abandoned.

Yikes! Does that mean you've lost all rights to your money? Nope. Luckily, by law, the mutual fund company must transfer your money to the state treasurer's office for the state of your last known address or the state in which the mutual fund company does business. This process is called escheatment and is most often associated with unclaimed assets left when a person dies without a will. The transfer can happen in 3 to 5 years after the mutual fund company loses contact with you or as much as 10 years later. If you don't claim the money, the state gets to keep it.

If you think you might have forgotten about funds that you left on deposit in a mutual fund company long ago, your first step should be to call that company. Often they can use their computer programs to search for your account using your Social Security number. If successful, the company can let you know whether the funds are still on deposit with them or if they've sent them to a state treasurer's office and to which office they've sent them.

Your next step would be to contact the state treasurer's office for each state you've lived in and find out how they handle abandoned accounts. Follow their procedures to do a search for any money abandoned from your prior accounts. A quick way to find the contact information for each state treasurer is at the National Association of State Treasurers (www.nast.net).

The fastest way to search for abandoned funds is UnclaimedFunds.org (www.unclaimedfunds.org), which manages an unclaimed money database that accesses 55 online searchable databases. These databases contain unclaimed property records from all over the United States. You will have to pay a fee to use this service, which ranges from $14.95 for a 90-day trial to $39.95 for a lifetime membership.

Requesting Old Statements

You may find that you need access to transaction history that is more than a year old. This happens most frequently when you are planning to sell funds and have to figure out your cost basis.

If you haven't done a good job of filing your year-end statements, you will probably be able to get a copy of older statements by requesting them through your mutual fund company. You may find it even easier if the company does let you access your records online. Often they also allow you access to an archival history of all your annual statements.

You may find that the company will charge you per statement requested. If all you need is to find out your average cost per share so you can calculate your cost basis, try to see if the company's accounting system is set up to do that for you. Many mutual fund companies are, and it will save you a lot of time and effort trying to figure out the cost of each of your shares purchased over many years.

The Least You Need to Know

- Always double-check your orders for mutual fund transactions to be sure you're buying the fund you intend. Verify your purchases quickly so you can correct any mistakes in a timely manner.

- You can handle many mutual fund transactions by telephone or online, but some changes do require a written notification.

- Mutual fund companies can make your account dormant and not send statements if they have been unable to reach you for a couple of years. After 5 to 10 years, they can consider your funds abandoned and turn them over to a state treasurer. All is not lost, and you may be able to recover the funds.

Chapter 11

Who's Watching the Funds?

In This Chapter

- The responsibilities of the board
- The need for independence
- Reasons for knowing fee structures

Few people who invest through mutual funds actually understand how those funds are governed, who picks the fund advisors and decides when it's time to make a change, who sets the fees you pay to those advisors to manage your funds, as well as who takes care of a myriad of other issues that impact your mutual fund returns. In this chapter, I take you behind the scenes to explain how a mutual fund is governed and how that governance impacts the cost of your mutual fund.

How Mutual Funds are Governed

Every mutual fund has a board of directors, just like a corporation—but how these board members are chosen is much different. The investment company that starts the fund initially appoints the mutual fund board. Mutual fund boards have four key responsibilities:

- To hire an investment advisor or portfolio manager to manage the funds being invested for shareholders.
- To oversee the day-to-day management of operations.
- To oversee the work of the investment advisor.
- To negotiate annual fees that the mutual fund shareholders will pay the advisor.

In addition to the board of directors, who oversee the operation of the funds, three other key entities manage the day-to-day operations of the funds:

- **Custodian** This person or company, holds the assets of the fund. If you buy or sell a fund, you correspond with the custodian of the fund.
- **Transfer Agent** The transfer agent has the direct responsibility to manage the individual accounts of each of the shareholders. In most cases the transfer agent is a wholly owned subsidiary of the mutual fund and operates out of the same offices of the fund.
- **Auditor** Hired by the board of directors, the auditor reviews the books of the mutual fund, usually on an annual basis.

When a director on the mutual fund board decides to leave, the board members nominate the replacement director. Mutual fund shareholders do not get to vote for their board members on an annual basis as do most corporate stockholders.

As we've seen when watching the mutual fund scandals of the past few years, there is some problem with this lack of shareholder input. Mutual fund chairmen and their boards have failed in their fiduciary responsibility to the shareholders of numerous funds. These directors lost money for their shareholders to scandals involving *market timing*, *directed brokerage*, and other practices that filled the pockets of mutual fund directors and companies, yet emptied the coffers that should have gone to mutual fund shareholders.

def•i•ni•tion

Some traders were given special privileges to trade mutual fund shares, after the closing price was already known. This is known as **market timing.** This practice cost the long-term mutual fund shareholders long-term profits.

Funds pay brokerage houses and mutual funds extra money under the table (in other words unknown to its mutual fund shareholders) to get special marketing and distribution benefits. This practice is known as **directed brokerage.** The fund company owners make money by attracting new shareholders who will pay fees, but the mutual fund shareholders pay the costs of that marketing.

Trying to fix the problems exposed during these scandals, the U.S. Securities and Exchange Commission approved new rules in 2004 related to mutual fund governance:

- The mutual fund chairman must be independent of the fund-management company. That sounds logical, doesn't it? The board of directors decides how much money the portfolio management company will be paid. Well, it's a most controversial rule and is still being fought by the mutual fund companies. I cover the problems of independence in the next section.

- At least 75 percent of the fund's directors should be independent (up from 50 percent previously). The controversy over this rule, which has lost to court challenges twice, we discuss in the next section.

- The board must assess its own effectiveness at least once a year.

- Independent directors (people not working for the investment company that owns the fund) must meet without the interested directors (mutual fund company executives including the investment advisor) at least once a quarter. The independent directors have the right to hire their own staff who do not report to the investment company that owns the fund.

- The fund must provide shareholders with better disclosure about the process used to select the investment advisor or portfolio manager and about the way fees are negotiated with the advisor.

Before I discuss the controversial rules regarding independence of the board of directors, I need to explain why this issue is so important. A mutual fund board of directors, who also work for the company that started the mutual fund, serve two masters—the people who buy the shares of the mutual fund are on one side of the equation and the people who buy shares of stock in the mutual fund company are on the other side. The interests of these two groups of investors often collide.

The mutual fund shareholders want the lowest possible fees, so the money they've invested in the mutual fund shares can grow very quickly. The people who bought shares of stock in the company that operates the mutual funds, such as T. Rowe Price, Morgan Stanley, or Merrill Lynch, want the operators of the fund to make the most money. As you can see, one side of the equation will always be hurt by any decision made.

If the board of directors negotiate lower fees, then the operators of the fund and fund advisors will make less money. The owners of stock in the mutual fund will suffer because the stock likely will have lower gains and lower dividends. If the directors instead allow fees charged to the mutual fund to go up, the mutual fund shareholders will see less growth in their portfolios because more of the gains in the assets held in the mutual fund portfolio will get eaten up by higher fees.

Controversy of Independence

You can understand from this issue of who wins—the mutual fund shareholders who want lower fees or the mutual company stockholders who want higher fees—that the rule that generates the greatest opposition from the mutual fund companies is the requirement for an independent chairman.

Can you imagine the discussion with the fund owners when there isn't an independent chairman? "What should the fee be this year?" "Well, we need $600 million to keep the company going." "Okay, that's fine."

Do you really think a person hired by the company is going to question the company president on what he wants? Only a truly independent chairman can question the fund owners and/or the investment advisors on the fees they want to charge and negotiate appropriately in the best interest of the mutual fund shareholders.

Most mutual fund companies opposed the independent-chairman requirement and the requirement for 75 percent of the mutual fund board to be independent directors. The issue was taken to court twice, and the SEC rule lost both times.

The first time the rule was tossed out because the court decided that the SEC did not properly consider the costs of the rule. When the SEC reaffirmed the rule with a cost assessment included, the court ruled the SEC must open its rule making to public comments on the commission's cost estimates. That comment period is still underway as I write this chapter.

During the public comment period, the SEC economists issued two reports that outline why it is so difficult to evaluate the benefits of the 75 percent independent director rule. While the SEC believes that with a greater proportion of independent directors there will more likely be improved attempts to negotiate lower fund fees and increased protection for mutual fund investors from trading abuses and other practices that costs mutual fund shareholders money, the SEC economists found it difficult to prove this theory with data available.

SEC economists have yet to find clear proof of the relationship between mutual fund performance and fund director independence. There simply aren't enough situations where mutual funds have predominately independent directors to generate the data that would help prove the SEC's position.

Yet New York Attorney General Eliot Spitzer (elected as New York governor in 2006 and responsible for exposing some of the worst mutual fund scandals) believes he showed why independent mutual fund boards were critical. David Brown, who headed Spitzer's investment protection bureau, said "there's not going to be significant reform in this industry until we get independent boards fighting for change. The way it's set up now is crazy—that the president of the fund management company is president of the board that's hiring [his firm]. He's on both sides of the table."

Fund Facts

We can see a prime example showing why independent mutual fund boards are essential in the case Spitzer brought against Richard S. Strong, who owned 85 percent of Strong Capital Management and chaired the Strong fund board. Strong finally settled civil charges against him by paying $60 million and personally apologizing to investors in his funds for letting them down. Regulators found that Strong made 1,400 short-term trades in funds he oversaw and netted $1.8 million in profits at the expense of his mutual funds investors—the people he was supposed to protect as a mutual fund board of directors chairman.

SEC Commissioner Roel Campos, at an open SEC Commission meeting where he voiced support for the SEC's continued push for independent boards said, "investigations by this Agency and other State Attorney Generals revealed that dozens of well known mutual fund families had turned large profits at the expense of mutual fund investors. Looking only at the top nine fund families, billions of dollars were literally stolen from mutual fund investors by executives who place their personal gain above the interests of their investors whom they were sworn to protect."

As part of cleaning up the market timing and late trading scandals, the SEC found that 16 of the 19 had management-affiliated or nonindependent chairmen at some time during the period these practices took place. Major fund families that faced action by the SEC included Invesco Funds, Franklin Templeton Funds, Janus, Putnam, Strong Funds, and MFS funds.

Fund Facts

In another scandal unearthed by the SEC in May 2005, the Commission announced a settlement with Citigroup Global Markets and Smith Barney Fund Management involving the lack of disclosure of significant fee discounts. Instead of passing on the negotiated discount to the mutual fund shareholders, the transfer agent affiliated with the mutual fund companies reaped nearly $100 million in profits at the expense of the fund shareholders. The funds involved did not have an independent chairman. Citigroup and Smith Barney paid over $200 million to settle the claim with the SEC.

At the writing of this book, the SEC was preparing its final papers regarding the economics of its rule requiring 75 percent of mutual fund directors be independent. Once those papers are released, SEC will open a comment period for 60 days. After that time, the SEC will issue a revised rule based on those comments, if necessary. The mutual fund industry could again decide to challenge any new rule in court once the SEC Commissions vote to implement the rule.

Opening the Window to Mutual Fund Fees

Why should all these battles about mutual fund director independence matter to you? Well, its all about money, whether the fees you pay to the mutual fund companies to manage your money are kept to a minimum or whether the mutual fund companies seek to make even more money by not passing on savings or making money with under-the-table deals and kickbacks.

In Chapter 4, I talked about the long-term impact of fees on your portfolio. Here I want to delve into the key issues that the mutual fund board of directors control and can change to save you money and allow your mutual fund accounts to grow even faster.

Morningstar's Managing Director, Don Phillips, testified before the Senate in February 2004 and sought five major changes that the SEC and mutual fund directors should make to protect mutual fund investors and help lower their mutual fund fees. Let's briefly look at each.

Fund Facts

Morningstar is the leading provider of independent research on mutual funds and other investment vehicles. Don Phillips started as an analyst at Morningstar in 1986 and was appointed managing director of Morningstar in 2000. He also serves on Morningstar's board of directors. He frequently testifies on behalf of Morningstar before Congress.

Stop Market Timing and Late Trading

Mutual funds must close the door to market timing and late trading abuses. The SEC has done a good job of taking steps to end this practice.

As the SEC and state Attorneys General expose the abuses, numerous mutual fund families have been forced to pay penalties. This is one area where I do think the SEC is taking a strong lead to correct the abuses.

End Direct Brokerage or Fully Disclose It

The SEC should eliminate the ability for mutual fund companies to enter into direct brokerage deals. If they decide to continue to allow this practice, then the mutual fund companies should be forced to better disclose pay-to-play arrangements.

In his Senate testimony, Phillips told senators that he believes these deals tilt the playing field against the investor who seeks brokerage advice. Rather than get independent advice, the broker's advice is tainted by the fees he makes behind the scenes with these deals. Many brokers steer the clients to the funds for which they will make the best commissions or fees.

At this point these behind-the-scenes marketing deals are still being kept a secret from mutual fund shareholders. Phillips believes that if the deals are not eliminated, the incentives brokers receive to steer clients to a particular fund should be fully disclosed prior to the investment being made.

I agree! And this is why I encourage you throughout this book to research funds on your own and purchase the funds you choose directly through the no-load mutual fund companies. That way you avoid having to pay secret costs.

Eliminate Soft-Dollar Payments

Soft-dollar arrangements give fund managers and mutual fund directors a way to dip into assets of the mutual fund to pay for research, trading systems, office furniture, and other services the mutual fund manager wants. While Phillips agrees that mutual fund companies do need to pay for these things, he believes they should be shown up front as part of the stated fee percentage so investors have a clear understanding what mutual fund management is costing them. Hiding these soft-dollar payments rather than including them in management fees keeps investors in the dark about the full cost of operations.

Discontinue or Restructure 12b-1

In Chapter 4, I discuss how 12b-1 fees are used to pay for marketing of fund shares. While there may be some minimal advantage to increasing the number of shareholders in a mutual fund and increasing its assets, the major advantage is to the fund company that will make additional profits by increasing the number of shareholders who must pay fees.

If 12b-1 fees are to be continued, Phillips believes these fees should be charged to the investors as part of their commissions if they decide to seek brokerage assistance in choosing and managing their funds. He does not think that all investors, even those who buy a mutual fund directly, should have to pay these marketing costs. As structured now, the 12b-1 fees, taken out yearly from a fund's total return, reduce the fund's return and yield annually.

In fact, Phillips testified to the Senate that Morningstar studies found that "managers of funds saddled with 12b-1 fees systematically take on greater risk than do managers of funds with lower expense ratios." If you do own a fund with 12b-1 fees charged annually, do your homework and find out if there is a similar fund that can meet your investing goal but is not saddled with these detrimental costs.

State Actual Fund Costs in Dollars

Right now mutual fund shareholders do not get a full disclosure of how much they are spending on mutual fund costs. These costs are only disclosed in an undefined percentage of assets. Phillips testified, and I agree entirely, that mutual funds should be required to disclose expenses in a detailed way with actual dollar costs rather than in a more secretive way using broad percentages.

By stating these fees in dollar costs, investors would have a better idea of what they are paying for to have their funds managed by a mutual fund company and could decide whether they are getting their money's worth. Armed with this greater detail, investors will be able to more accurately measure the value of the services they are paying for with each company, compare the services and their costs, and make informed decisions about which mutual fund is being operated more effectively and efficiently. Phillips also believes that if these costs are disclosed for mutual funds, they should also be disclosed for exchange-traded funds, variable annuities, and separately managed accounts to even the playing field. In addition to these monetary changes, Phillips also called for changes to the way the SEC regulates mutual funds, the accountability of mutual fund directors to their shareholders, the disclosure of trading by mutual fund managers, the full disclosure of fund manager compensation, and the improvement of the asset holdings in mutual fund portfolios.

Make Mutual Fund Regulation a Priority

Phillips and many other consumer groups, including the Consumer Federation of America (www.consumerfed.org) and Fund Democracy (www.funddemocracy.com) regularly testify in Congress and write letters to urge more scrutiny of the mutual fund industry by the SEC and by Congress. Phillips testified that the SEC should "prioritize mutual fund regulation among the numerous tasks it handles. Mutual funds are too important to the country's savings to be a back-burner issue with regulators."

Thanks to the work of Spitzer, the SEC is finally on the bandwagon and appears to be taking more significant actions to rein in mutual funds and regulate their managers and directors. Hopefully the actions we've seen over the past few years will not be in vain, and significant gains can be made for the individual investor.

Improve Accountability to Shareholders

Have you heard from your mutual fund's board of directors lately? Or ever? Too often mutual fund investors will answer "no" to both of these questions. In fact, mutual fund directors have much more contact with the fund's manager than they do with any fund shareholders. Phillips even testified at the Senate hearing that he's heard from directors of public corporate boards that they receive regular letters from their shareholders, yet the same people who serve on mutual fund boards never hear from their shareholders.

Why do you think there is so little contact? In most cases I bet you don't even know who serves on the board of directors for your mutual fund. Directors are rarely even discussed in annual reports to shareholders. Phillips believes this must change and calls for more direct contact and accountability to mutual fund shareholders.

Phillips believes that an independent mutual fund board chairman should be responsible for reporting annually to fund shareholders as part of the annual report. This report should include the steps the board took during the year to review the manager's performance, as well as the contract the fund has with the manager. He also believes that directors should have much greater oversight regarding the communications between mutual fund managers and mutual fund shareholders.

Increased visibility, combined with increased independence, should give mutual fund shareholders a better voice in how mutual funds are managed and what fees are charged.

Better Disclosure of Trading by Mutual Fund Managers

If you hold shares of stock in a public company, you can get detailed information about the number of shares held by the corporate executives, as well as their trading activity. Often this information can give stock investors a heads up. If executives are selling shares, there may be trouble ahead, or if buying shares, the executive believes in the long-term future of the company. Many people watch the trading moves of executives as one of the clues for future potential of a stock.

Mutual fund shareholders don't have access to this type of information about the mutual fund manager or its directors. While it's easy to understand why a fund manager would not want to be required to disclose his individual trading of fund shares, recent scandals show why this information should be available. As mentioned earlier, Strong Funds's owner, who engaged in market timing of his own mutual fund shares, was forced to pay $60 million in penalties by the SEC to settle the case.

Disclosure can be a powerful deterrent to this type of behavior. Clearly investors, as well as the SEC, need to be able to keep a more careful watch on mutual fund managers and directors.

Increase Disclosure of Fund Manager and Director Compensation

This same principal of disclosure should also apply to compensation for managers. If you own stock in a public company, you know exactly how much the chief executives make and how any bonuses are calculated. If you own shares in mutual funds, you don't have a clue.

Why should this matter? A fund manager's incentives could greatly impact the decisions that manager makes about a mutual fund's portfolio. For example, if the incentives are based on short-term annual gains in the fund, then the manager will seek to meet or exceed the required benchmarks to get his bonus. But if instead the bonuses are based on a longer-term five-year record, the manager will seek to meet or exceed those benchmarks. This could have a great impact on the long-term gains a mutual fund investor might expect to get.

Increased disclosure of compensation packages will help mutual fund shareholders make better choices about which funds meet their own long-term goals. You can be almost certain that any manager will seek to meet or exceed his benchmarks to earn his best bonus potential.

Improve Disclosure of the Asset Holdings in Mutual Fund Portfolios

Another critical piece of information mutual fund shareholders need is more frequent disclosure of the assets in a mutual fund portfolio. Right now mutual funds are only required to publish a mutual fund's holding every six months. Mutual fund managers believe they need this secrecy to control the information about their trades.

While it's true that a manager needs to make his investing decisions in private, those decisions are no longer private ones shortly after any major moves are made in the marketplace. An increased volume of trading in any stock gets noticed quickly in the marketplace.

Phillips believes the mutual fund manager can keep the needed privacy for initial trading, yet disclose mutual fund holdings more often. He thinks a monthly disclosure, possibly using the fund's Internet website, would satisfy the need for disclosure without hurting the manager's portfolio moves.

Why should this matter to you? The issue came to light in the early 2000s when investors thought they were investing in well-diversified mutual funds and found out, after the market crashed, that their mutual fund managers had invested their portfolios too heavily in risky technology stocks.

If monthly portfolio disclosure had been required, these investors would have seen the shift to technology stocks and could have gotten out if that choice by their mutual fund manager was a riskier move than they wanted to take. They could have sold their mutual fund and moved it to a safer investor. By not knowing about these changes until after the market crashed, mutual fund investors lost billions of dollars.

As you learn more about who controls your mutual funds and how that control can impact the success or failure of your mutual fund portfolio, you will want to keep up on all these mutual fund governance issues. One of the best ways to do that is through the website Fund Democracy (www. funddemocracy.com). All letters and Congressional testimony about key SEC actions or Congressional legislation are posted on the site.

The Least You Need to Know

- Find out who serves on the board of directors for your mutual funds, and don't hesitate to contact them if you have a question about how the mutual fund is being managed.

- Mutual fund boards make key decisions about how your money is managed, including who the manager will be and how much that manager will be paid.

- Mutual fund boards need greater independence so they can be more responsible to you, the investor, rather than just to the company that hires them.

- All mutual fund shareholders need greater disclosure about fees, manager compensation, and trading, as well as asset holding.

Glossary

account fee   This fee is imposed by some funds on investors to pay the costs of maintaining their accounts. For example, accounts below a specified dollar amount may have to pay an account fee.

back-end load   One way brokers are compensated for selling a fund is a back-end load (also known as a "deferred sales charge"). Investors pay this load when they redeem (or sell) their mutual fund shares.

capital appreciation   This is the increase in the current market value of your holdings. The market value is the price you can get for your asset if you want to sell it today.

capital gains   This is the amount of profit you make when you sell an asset. For example, if you buy a share of stock for $10 and sell it for $15, your capital gain is $5 minus any fees or commissions you paid to buy and sell that stock.

classes   Load funds are grouped in several different type classes, such as Class A, Class B, Class C, and so on. Each class invests in the same investment portfolio and has the same investment objectives and policies. The key difference between the classes is how shareholder services and loads are paid. There are also different annual operating fee ratios, so you will see different long term results for each of the classes.

closed-end mutual funds   These are funds in which a fixed number of shares are sold at an initial public offering (IPO). After that IPO, these funds are traded more like stocks than are open-end mutual funds.

Contingent Deferred Sales Load   One type of back-end load, this load (CDSL) is dependent upon the amount of time you hold the fund. Usually the percentage of the fee is reduced each year that you hold the fund until the fee becomes zero.

conversion   If you buy a mutual fund with classes, some funds allow you to automatically change from one class to another. You usually do this to take advantage of lower annual expenses.

deferred sales charge   *See* "back-end load."

distribution (12b-1) fees   Fees in this expense category, which are identified in most prospectuses as "12b-1 fees," are paid out of fund assets to cover distribution or marketing expenses.

diversification   This is a strategy used to reduce your exposure to risk by holding a variety of investments, such as stocks, bonds, and real estate, which don't usually move up or down in value in the same direction at the same time.

dividends   These are paid by a corporation to their stockholders based on the profits earned in a given year. This is the way corporations share their profits with the people who own their stock.

exchange fee   This is a fee that some funds charge to shareholders who want to exchange their shares from one fund to another within the same mutual fund family.

exchange-traded funds (ETFs)   These are funds that track a specific stock exchange index, such as the S&P 500 index. ETFs bundle together the securities in that index and trade the package in the same way that stock is bought and sold.

expense ratio   This ratio represents the fund's total annual operating expenses (including management fees, distribution (12b-1) fees, and other expenses). It will be calculated as a percentage of average net assets.

Federal Deposit Insurance Company (FDIC)
This agency protects the first $100,000 per depositor in most banks. Be sure your bank displays the FDIC symbol and indicates your checking and savings accounts are protected.

fee-based   This type of financial advisor charge sets fees based on the work you ask them to do. Their fee can be based on an hourly charge or can be based on a percentage of the assets you want them to manage.

front-end load   This is the sales charge that you must pay to cover the salesperson (broker's) commission when you pay a fund that requires this fee be paid when you buy the mutual fund. The front-end load fee reduces the amount that is used to purchase mutual fund shares.

hedge funds These funds are usually used solely by wealthy individuals and institutions that want to find a money manager who will use aggressive and riskier investing strategies. Most hedge funds are exempt from many of the rules governing mutual funds. Investors usually need at least $100,000 to get into a hedge fund.

index fund This describes a type of mutual fund whose assets are managed using a mathematical model to match the performance of a particular stock or bond market index, such as the S&P 500 Composite Stock Price Index, the Russell 2000 Index, or the Wilshire 5000 Total Market Index.

investment advisor If you seek professional help to invest in mutual funds, this is the person who provides that help. This person receives compensation for helping you decide on which stocks, bonds, or mutual funds to pick. Sometimes investment advisors also manage stock or bond portfolios, including mutual fund portfolios.

load *See* "sales charge."

management fee Professional managers must be paid, and the management fees that are paid to a fund's investment advisors cover their professional fees for portfolio management. Sometimes there also are other management fees payable to the advisor's affiliates. Administrative fees directly related to portfolio management also fit under this category.

market index   A market index measures the performance of a specific "basket" of stocks representing a particular market or sector of the U.S. stock market or the economy. For example, the Dow Jones Industrial Average (DJIA), which is an index that includes 30 large corporations or "blue chip" U.S. stocks, is a popular index of industrial corporations.

mutual fund   Mutual funds pool the money of many individual investors and then invest those funds in a variety of ways.

mutual fund family   This is a group of funds managed under the same company umbrella. Some well-known families include Vanguard, Fidelity, and T. Rowe Price.

NAV (Net Asset Value)   At the end of each day, a mutual fund's value is calculated by totaling the fund's assets minus its liabilities and divided by the number of outstanding shares, which is called the NAV or net asset value. The U.S. Securities and Exchange Commission requires funds to calculate the NAV at least once daily.

no-load fund   You buy this fund without having to pay a sales charge. No-load funds may charge fees that are not related to sales loads or commissions. You will have to pay annual operating expenses for a no-load mutual fund.

open-end company   This is the legal name for a mutual fund, which is a type of investment company.

operating expenses   This represents the costs of running a mutual fund company including management fees, distribution (12b-1) fees, and other expenses, which are charged annually to the fund's shareholders. Operating expenses are taken out of the mutual fund share portfolio before the year-end rate of return is calculated.

portfolio manager This is the person in charge of picking the investments for the fund and managing those investments. When you buy a mutual fund, what you are really buying is the professional management skills of the portfolio manager. The portfolio manager is the one that buys the fund's assets.

preferred stocks This stock type has a specified dividend that must be paid before common stock holders get their dividends. Preferred stock holders do not have voting rights at the annual meeting for the company.

prospectus This is a legal document that describes the mutual fund to prospective investors. The prospectus contains information about the mutual fund's costs, investment objectives, risks, and performance.

purchase fee Some mutual funds charge a purchase fee to their shareholders when they buy shares of the fund. This fee is paid to the mutual fund company and not to the broker or mutual fund supermarket that initiated the sale. The purchase fee covers the fund's costs associated with the purchase.

redemption fee Some mutual funds charge a redemption fee to shareholders when they sell their shares. This fee is usually a percentage deducted from the redemption proceeds, but it's not a sales load.

sales charge   These fees and commissions are paid to the broker, advisor, insurance company, or other entity from whom you buy your mutual fund. These funds are subtracted from your investment before your account with the mutual fund company is opened or subtracted when you sell your funds before you receive your money.

shareholder service fees   Some funds charge fees to cover the costs of responding to investor inquiries and provide investors with information about their investments.

total annual fund operating expense   Each year the mutual fund totals all operating expenses. The total of a fund's annual fund operating expenses is expressed as a percentage of the fund's average net assets. You'll find this total in the fund's fee table in the prospectus.

Resources

Government and Private Agencies

You can count on three key agencies for solid information about mutual funds—the U.S. Securities and Exchange Commission, the National Association of Securities Dealers, and the Investment Company Institute.

U.S. Securities and Exchange Commission (SEC)

The SEC is the primary government regulator for mutual funds. You can find excellent investor resources on their website at www.sec.gov/investor.shtml.

One of the best tools for mutual funds is the mutual fund fees and expenses calculator (www.sec.gov/investor/tools/mfcc/mfcc-int.htm). Any time you are considering new funds, always compare costs and fees, which can be the biggest drag on your mutual fund profits.

If you need to file a complaint with the SEC, you can do so online at https://tts.sec.gov/acts-ics/do/complaint.

If you prefer to contact the SEC by telephone or e-mail, here is the contact information:

- SEC Toll-Free Investor Information Service: 1-800-SEC-0330. Use this number to obtain free publications and investor alerts, learn how to file a complaint, and contact the SEC for other investor questions.

- Contact by mail:
  SEC Headquarters
  100 F Street, NE
  Washington, DC 20549
  Office of Investor Education and Assistance

National Association of Securities Dealers (NASD)

For more than 60 years, the NASD has served as a private-sector provider of financial regulatory services to help bring integrity to the markets and confidence to investors. Under federal law, virtually every securities firm doing business with the U.S. public is a member of this private, not-for-profit organization. Roughly 5,050 brokerage firms, over 171,790 branch offices, and more than 662,150 registered securities representatives come under NASD jurisdiction.

You can find extensive investor information on its website at www.nasd.com. The NASD offers a mutual fund expense analyzer and a mutual fund breakpoint search, which helps you find discounts and waivers for load mutual funds.

You will also find investor alerts, a place to check on the background of brokers, and an investor complaint center. You can find the investor complaint center for the NASD at www.nasd. com/InvestorInformation/InvestorProtection/ InvestorComplaintCenter/index.htm. If you have trouble using this link, go to www.nasd.com, and click on the link to Investor Complaint Center. You'll find it on the front page of the website in the right column titled "Investor Information."

Investment Company Institute

The Investment Company Institute (ICI), which is the national association of U.S. investment companies (mutual funds), was found in 1940. Its membership as of October 2006 included 8,821 mutual funds, 654 closed-end funds, 234 exchange-traded funds, and four sponsors of unit investment trusts. Its mutual fund members serve 89.5 million individual shareholders and manage $9.468 trillion in investor assets.

In addition to finding key statistics about mutual fund investing at its website (www.ici.org), you'll also find excellent mutual fund investing educational resources at www.ici.org/funds/inv.

Mutual Funds and Taxes

While no one really enjoys learning about the taxes due, mutual fund owners do have some unique rules they must understand. The best publication for learning about mutual funds and taxes is IRS

Publication 564 (www.irs.gov/publications/p564/index.html), "Mutual Fund Distributions.

Mutual Fund News and Analysis Websites

You'll find a lot of information on the web about mutual funds; three of the best sites to watch regularly are Morningstar, Marketwatch, and FundAlarm.

Morningstar

Morningstar (www.morningstar.com) provides excellent analysis and news coverage about mutual funds. You will also find many useful tools for screening funds and managing your mutual fund portfolio.

Marketwatch

Marketwatch is an excellent investor news source provided by Dow Jones, which also publishes the *Wall Street Journal*. When you get to the site, click on the tab for "Mutual Funds and ETFs" to find excellent coverage of the industry. You may also want to explore the "Personal Finance" tab for stories about good investing strategies.

FundAlarm

FundAlarm (www.fundalarm.com) is a website that helps you decide when it's time to sell a fund rather than when it's time to buy. The managers of

FundAlarm seek to alert you to problems with specific mutual funds. You can sign up for a free e-mail that alerts to updates on the website.

Independent Financial Advisor

If you'd like to work with a financial advisor, the best way to find one is through recommendations from a friend or family member. If you don't know anyone who can recommend a good financial advisor, you can locate one near you through the Financial Planning Association (www.fpanet.org/public). At their website you'll find articles about how to pick a financial advisor, as well as a database you can search to find an advisor that will best meet your needs.

Top No-Load Mutual Funds

The no load mutual fund companies that consistently have top performing mutual funds in their family include:

- Dodge & Cox Funds (www.dodgeandcox. com) or call 1-800-621-3979
- Fidelity (www.fidelity.com) or call 1-800-544-9797
- Janus (www.janus.com) or call 1-800-525-0020
- Oakmark (www.oakmark.com) or call 1-800-625-6275
- TIAA-CREF (www.tiaa-cref.org/products/mutual) or call 1-800-223-1200

- T. Rowe Price (www.troweprice.com) or call
  1-800-638-5660

- Vanguard (www.vanguard.com) or call
  1-800-997-2798

Top Mutual Fund Supermarkets and Discount Brokers

- Charles Schwab (www.schwab.com)—
  Schwab developed the first mutual fund
  supermarket. To find its mutual fund supermarket, which is called "OneSource," click
  on the "Investment Products" tab, then on
  the "Mutual Funds" tab.

- E-Trade (us.etrade.com/e/t/invest/
  mfgettingstarted)

- TD Waterhouse (www.tdameritrade.com/
  researchideas/mutualfundsetfs/fundFamilies.
  html)

Two large no-load mutual fund companies that provide their customers with the ability to buy funds,
or even stocks, through their supermarkets include:

- Vanguard (www.vanguard.com)—To find
  the mutual fund supermarket, when you get
  to the website, click on "Go to the site."
  Then click on the link to "Brokerage services
  for investing in stocks, bonds, and non-
  Vanguard funds."

- Fidelity (www.fidelity.com)—Fidelity calls
  its supermarket the FundsNetwork. Find it
  by clicking on the link to "Mutual Funds" in
  the column on the left side of the page titled
  "Our Products." On the mutual fund page
  you will see a link "Explore more than 4,500
  funds."

Trying to Find Lost Mutual Funds

The fastest way to search for abandoned funds is
to use UnclaimedFunds.org (www.unclaimedfunds.
org), which manages an unclaimed money database
that accesses 55 online searchable databases. These
databases contain unclaimed property records from
all over the United States. You pay a fee to use this
service, which ranges from $14.95 for a 90 day trial
to $39.95 for a lifetime membership.

Recommended Books

If you'd like to read additional information about
mutual funds, two books we recommend are:

Bogle, John C. *Common Sense on Mutual Funds: New
Imperatives for the Intelligent Investor.* New York:
John Wiley & Sons, 2000.

Bogle, who started Vanguard Mutual Funds, provides excellent information about mutual fund
investment strategy and the importance of being
patient. He repeatedly stresses time as a basic tenet

for investing, listing these simple rules: "Time is your friend." "Impulse is your enemy." "Stay the course." He also blasts fund managers, who have become marketers rather than managers.

The Morningstar Guide to Mutual Funds: 5-Star Strategies for Success. New York: John Wiley & Sons, 2004.

This book quickly became a *Business Week* and *Wall Street Journal* bestseller. You'll find solid constructive mutual fund investing advice by Morningstar, who used its nearly two decades of research and analysis to develop excellent common sense strategies to investing in mutual funds.

Liberman, Gail, and Alan Lavine. *The Complete Idiot's Guide to Making Money with Mutual Funds.* Indianapolis: Alpha Books, 2003.

Koch, Edward T., Debra DeSalvo, and Joshua A. Kennon. *The Complete Idiot's Guide to Investing, Third Edition.* Indianapolis: Alpha Books, 2005.

Index

N

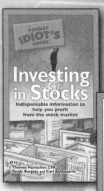